# Sherpa in My Backpack

A Guide to International Social Work Practicum
Exchanges and Study Abroad Programs

# Sherpa in My Backpack

A Guide to International Social Work Practicum
Exchanges and Study Abroad Programs

by

Karen Schwartz
Linda Kreitzer
Constance A. Barlow
Laurie Macdonald

de Sitter Publications
111 Bell Dr., Whitby, ON,
L1N 2T1, Canada

**Library and Archives Canada**
**Cataloguing in Publication**

Schwartz, Karen, Kreitzer, Linda, Barlow, Constance A., Macdonald, Laurie
   Sherpa in my backpack : a guide to international social work practicum exchanges and study abroad programs / written by Karen Schwartz, Linda Kreitzer, Constance A. Barlow, Laurie Macdonald

Includes bibliographical references and index.

**ISBN 978-1-897160-84-8**

**de Sitter Publications**
111 Bell Dr., Whitby, ON,
L1N 2T1, Canada
289-987-0656
info@desitterpublications.com

# Contents

# Foreword

As human services professions move towards globalizing their activities and extending their research agendas to the wider world context, there is a growing interest in the international aspect of education, scholarship, and practice. Social work has a long standing tradition in international exchanges that spans nearly 100 years. Community organizer and social activist Jane Addams, who was instrumental in the settlement house movement in the United States, participated in possibly the first international exchange by visiting Toynbee Hall, a settlement house in London in 1904 (Link & Vogrincic, 2012). While our educational backgrounds are firmly rooted in social work and we will use specific examples from the field of social work, we believe many aspects of this book can inform students and faculty members from related human services professions who are engaged in international exchanges.

Diverse perspectives are represented in this book. As authors, we share our personal views, based on our experience with international social work exchange students and our work on several international development projects. One of these enterprises was a five year research project entitled, "Evaluation of Social Work Field Education," which received ethics clearance from University of Calgary and Carleton University. The primary data source for this study was a Canadian/EU social work exchange funded by HRSDC and Eurasmus between four cities in Canada (Calgary, Kelowna, Montreal, and Ottawa) and four countries in the EU (Austria, Belgium, Finland, and Poland). Additionally some of the authors initiated exchanges involving students who completed international exchanges in Australia and India. We also share comments made by students in their journals, on feedback forms, in web based discussion groups and other assignments. Some of the students are Canadians who traveled abroad and some are international students who came to Canada. We are forever grateful to all of them and applaud their courage and wisdom. If you are interested in reading more about these projects, other publications by the authors are listed in the references at the end of the book.

As social work academics, we have organized and supervised international social work internships for much of our careers and have witnessed the transformative nature of these exchanges. We come together to share these stories with you in the hope that it will enhance your international experience. Our main goal is to create a manual that encourages you as a student to proceed with an international exchange and to aid you in planning and achieving a successful experience. As well, we also hope to assist faculty members as they guide students through this process.

We operate from the following four assumptions:

1.  International exchanges are a rich and potentially transformative experience, but these exchanges can also be potentially horrifying and traumatic if students are not adequately prepared and supported.
2.  Gaps exist in the published literature on international exchanges, and in particular the voices of students are limited.
3.  Self-reflection is critical to a successful internship.
4.  Social justice and anti-oppressive perspectives are foundational to international exchanges.

International education is evolving as many students in the human services undertake international exchanges and from this background various models have developed. For example, many western universities are developing short-term "study abroad" programs for students such that they can complete a portion of their internship hours in a foreign country. An internship may consist of an excursion with faculty escorts to a country for a period lasting from one day to several weeks, at times as an "alternate spring break activity." Reciprocal arrangements are enabling students from developing countries to earn internship hours at human service agencies, NGOs, and governmental organizations affiliated with western universities and colleges. In keeping with the move towards internationalization, **semester long exchange** opportunities are being offered abroad.

While there are significant differences between short term and semester long exchanges, students and instructors who engage in international endeavors note the lack of resources to guide them in developing and maintaining various forms of international exchanges and in supporting and instructing students. *Sherpa in My Backpack* is a unique resource that fills a gap in the literature on international exchanges, internships, practica and short-term study abroad programs. This seminal book in the area of education offers a comprehensive guide for students, and informs faculty members and field instructors who are participating in international exchanges, in the following ways:

- It offers **practical** guidelines for developing international exchanges, and for creating university-based infrastructures to support these endeavors.
- It provides detailed information on how to prepare students for international study and how to create an environment, both virtually and face-to-face, that supports integrative learning.
- It represents the **student experiences** in the form of case studies and personal narratives. The data source for this aspect of the book was from a five year research project, by one of the authors, which examined the experiences of social work students in international field placements, as well as from the five year Canada-Euro project.
- It represents the **university-based experience** through the use of case studies based on real-

life examples derived from the experience of the authors, who, for many years, have been involved in international social work practicum internships.

- It can be adapted to **on-line** or face-to-face settings.
- It presents **learning activities** that can be adapted to a range of settings.

Finally, we hope that this practical guide will prevent mistakes that we made during these processes and that it will foster productive international exchanges with as few headaches as possible. We invite you into the world of the international exchange and wish the best as your faculty, students, and field advisors embark on this exciting adventure.

# Introduction

The Sherpas are Eastern peoples, coming from Tibet, who have settled in the high mountain valleys of Nepal for over 600 years. Around 30,000 live in Nepal today and for many, their main source of economic stability is the climbing and tourism industry. A Sherpa is hired by climbing expeditions to navigate and guide the mountaineers up the mountain safely. These Sherpas are renowned for their climbing knowledge, which makes a difference between a successful climb and one that fails, thus putting the mountaineers in danger. We named our book "Sherpa in My Backpack" using this metaphor in honour of these amazing people who are hired to guide people up and down the mountains and to help in times when mountaineers are stuck and need to know how to get out of a situation. This guidebook is written for students, but is also appropriate for faculty and practitioners to guide them into the world of international exchanges so that they come out on top and have positive experiences. It can enable faculty to be better academic Sherpas who help guide students through this process. Understanding that not all exchanges will be the perfect climb, this guidebook will help people through the difficult terrain of international exchanges. Like climbers flocking to climb Everest and in need of Sherpas, more and more people are interested in international exchanges and need effective guidelines to help them along the way.

Social work educators worldwide have consistently embraced the belief that field exchanges, commonly referred to as field placements, are a necessary element of professional education. The general objective of field placements is to assist students in learning, applying, and integrating social work values, knowledge, and skills through the provision of learning experiences offered in the field exchanges. The primary goals of field placements are the development of the students' professional identity, reciprocal learning with colleagues, and the integration of theory and practice. A partnership between a community social service agency and a school of social work provides the infrastructure for achieving this goal.

There is a growing interest in the international aspect of social work education, scholarship, and practice as the profession moves towards globalizing its activities and extending its research agenda to the wider context. Social workers are more aware today of the global impact of social problems and the relations between local problems and the global context. In this role, social workers need to be more effective players in order to respond to the realities of global interdependency (Ife, 2007). There is a move to provide students with opportunities to develop attitudes and skills required in international exchanges and curriculum content in many schools is drawing more attention to developing a critical analysis of a world context.

The social work profession is also gaining recognition around the world. In many Asian/Pacific countries such as Vietnam, Japan, India, and New Zealand, social services and educational programs are being developed and extended. In Africa, the profession is taking on a new life as more countries work from a social development economic perspective. Also, social work is undergoing a period of rapid transition in many Eastern European and subcontinent countries like the former Yugoslavia, the former Soviet Union, Czech State, Slovakia, and Hungary. As a result of these developments, international exchanges are evolving as many students undertake international field placements. Western universities are developing "study abroad" programs for students such that they can complete a portion of their field placement hours in a foreign country. Reciprocal arrangements, although not as equitable (Hokenstad, 2012) are enabling students from developing countries to earn field placement hours at social service agencies affiliated with western universities and colleges. As universities are embracing an internationalization policy, exchange opportunities are being offered abroad more now than ever before.

## Why an International Exchange in Social Work or other Human Services?

Why is an international exchange important to the growth of a social work student? One student describes the importance of her learning through an international exchange:

> I found that I had a narrow, North American view of social work or "helping." As I was permitted to take part in a culture that does not share the same understanding of helping, I found that my conception of social work broadened and opened to include other ways of being and knowing. The importance of one's sense of belonging, connectedness to others, and family (beyond blood relations) to healing and wellness became very clear to me.

Besides broadening our horizons and perceiving beyond our culture, there are five other benefits of an international exchange.

### Five benefits of an international exchange:

1. It challenges assumptions about definitions of social problems.
2. It invites considerations of alternative interventions.
3. It leads to creative thinking about human service practice in your home country.
4. It prompts consideration of a broader definition of social work practice than that which is promoted in the home culture.
5. It facilitates networking between social workers throughout the world in relation to friendships, strong linkages, and partnerships.

Another student wrote:

> The experience did make a difference in my personal life. It really opened me up to people I never thought that I could relate to.

There is increasing recognition of the importance of international field placements and their role in developing social work practice so that it may bring different perspectives about what we can see, what should be avoided, and what should be understood (Barlow, 2007; Healy & Link, 2012; Lager & Mathiesen, 2012; Lyons, 2006; Payne & Askeland, 2008; Razack, 2002). Understanding power issues between countries and different peoples (for example, indigenous peoples) has to be prominent in preparing students from western countries going to countries that have been colonized and are continually colonized through economic and political systems. Razack (2000) and Kreitzer & Wilson (2009) raise some important questions about international social work field placements: Who is applying? To what countries? Reasons behind their choices? Are any from the "south"? What are the implications? These are fundamental questions that should be asked by faculty, field coordinators, and students when engaging in the planning of international field placements. "Student mobility requires careful preparation and plans for support, as well as attention to the power imbalances inherent in existing global structures and interpersonal relationships" (Hokenstad, 2012, p. 173).

A common theme is that international social work field placements doesn't just happen; it must be fostered, encouraged, and developed at home. The same is true for other human services. Dominelli and Bernard (2003, p. 26) outline four issues regarding international student exchanges and field placements:

1. lack of theory on the needs of the students to help them link their theory to practice needs
2. applicability of the experience in their local (home) practice;

3. predominance still, of English language publications, theorising of international developments; and
4. dominance, still, of western models of practice and English language (see Wilson & Whitmore, 2000).

These are some of the theoretical considerations that frame international exchanges. However, beyond these considerations, some very practical guidance as to the role of the faculty, field coordinator, and student is needed. This guide attempts to fill in the gaps with practical advice and guidance in developing and supporting students in international field placements, as well as offering activities that help students relate theory to practice. In other words, this is what we wish someone had told us before we started.

This practical guide is divided into eight chapters. Each chapter represents a stage in the process of organising international field placements. Each chapter starts with a brief introduction and ends with some reflective questions. Students' stories are included to give a hands-on perspective.

In **Chapter 1**, we provide a brief background of colonialism and present day hegemony of western culture and its impact on many countries of the world. Through the lens of anti-oppressive social work practice, a brief discussion follows concerning the responsibility of students and their academic Sherpas to act and practice in an anti-oppressive manner. Examples of how this can be done, including student examples, will end this chapter. Again this can be applied to all human service practice.

**Chapter 2** begins with how students can organize an international exchange, and directs students to areas that require particular attention.

**Chapter 3** is an outline of how an academic Sherpa is crucial to the success of an international exchange. We discuss the various important roles of Sherpas are their interactions with various stakeholders including the university, community, and partners. Examples are provided from one university as well as anecdotes from students about what was helpful to the process.

**Chapter 4** assists students in identifying learning goals and provides helpful activities for students to meet these goals. Some of the suggested activities are thinking about the basic information that you want to have about the country that you are travelling to, making presentations about the culture of your host country, and writing about critical incidents that occur during your exchange.

**Chapter 5** contains information on preparation for going overseas, cultural issues, and what to expect when doing your international exchange.

In **Chapter 6** we highlight some of the feelings that students experience during their time abroad. Also discussed are issues concerning sexual harassment and how to handle this difficult situation, challenges within the agency, dealing with trauma and illness, and handling intimate relationships while abroad.

In **Chapter 7** we address coming home and cultural re-integration, which is one of the least written about experiences in international exchange. We look at the experiences of students as they return home, apply for jobs, and try and integrate their overseas experience into their life back home.

**Chapter 8** is a summary of the process of setting up, actively facilitating an exchange, and things to consider as you re-integrate into your own culture.

We close this chapter with a student's comments about the benefits of an international exchange:

From doing my placement in Finland I gained a variety of experiences that would not have been available to me if I had done my field placement in Canada. I was able to be part of an organization that offers a wide range of programs and services, an organization that has been established

*continued...*

in Finland for over one hundred years and is known for its outstanding commitment to clients and communities. I was able to take part in a variety of units within this organization, giving me a multi-dimensional view of the organization and how it all works together and as separate entities. I was able to educate people on the differences between Canada and Finland, in a cultural and social services sense, as well as be educated about Finland's culture and society. I was able to take part in cultural practices and share some of my own from Canada, creating bonds with clients, workers, and friends through our differences and often through our similarities. I would encourage students who have the opportunity to do placements abroad to take advantage of this once in a lifetime chance. I got to be part of a different culture, learn about the similarities and differences between Finland and Canada, help clients become more confident in their English speaking skills, compare the social service sectors of two countries, travel throughout Finland and experience personal and professional growth.

This international exchange guide book is intended to be the Sherpa for international exchanges.

## Reflection Questions

1. Has anyone at your university emerged as a Sherpa who will help you organize the international exchange in which you wish to participate?
2. Does your human service program offer a course on the impact of globalization on your field of study? Have issues of globalization been integrated into any of your courses?
3. If not, how aware are you of issues of globalization and human service?
4. If so, do you need to further educate yourself about any of these issues?

# Chapter 1

## Anti-Oppressive Perspectives in International Exchanges

We live in a world in which power imbalance is constant among individuals, cultures and countries. Historical factors of conflict, domination, exploitation, colonization, modernization and globalization have set the stage for the current imbalances of power. We do not choose where we are born and for many people, where they are born and the beliefs they choose to own, may not conform to dominant cultures in the world. If these people, because of their beliefs, are threatened by the dominate culture, they often do not have a choice to move where they want to live in the world, even if this means that they and their family's lives are at stake. Quite simply, some of us are privileged in this world and others spend their lives trying to survive under oppressive situations and under the dominance of others.

Colonialists exploited and oppressed many cultures, and the consequences are felt today in parts of Africa, the Americas, Asia, and the Middle East. However, Freire (1997) sees every human being as a possible oppressor and one who is oppressed. Within each of these regions, ethnic cultures are oppressing and being oppressed, by inside and outside forces, with the result that many indigenous peoples' languages and cultures are becoming extinct. The widening gap between rich and poor, xenophobia, war and conflicts, genocide, and exploitation of women and children all seem overwhelming and a little unreal to privileged people who have not experienced these events. The belief that the western world is the land of milk and honey permeates non-western cultures and sets up a situation in which immigrants arriving to a western country are inevitably disappointed and find life harder than they expected. When people from wealthier countries travel to a lower income country, they are often tourists who, if not consciously wishing to meet local people, will retreat to a paradise of hotels and beaches that are not accessible to the local population, thus avoiding the realities of local conditions. Beliefs about different countries and people, whether real or unreal, are a challenge when studying abroad. Anti-oppressive practice (AOP) challenges our beliefs and is crucial to how we practice. So how does AOP play out in an international exchange?

## Anti-Oppressive Perspective

According to Baines (2011), anti-oppressive perspective examines the "complexity of today's social problems in the context of multiple oppressions and the growing need for fundamental reorganization of all levels of society" in order to end oppression, (p.4). She describes a number of core themes in AOP social work practice that are important for international exchanges. We will address four of the themes identified by Baines (2011).

### Four themes of anti-oppressive practice for international exchanges

1. Macro- and micro-social relations generate oppression.
2. Everyday experience is shaped by multiple oppressions.
3. Participatory approaches are necessary between [all people working in the human services with clients].
4. Self-reflective practice and on-going social analysis are essential components of AOP. (pp. 4-7)

## 1. Macro- and micro-social relations

The first core theme suggests that social relations that generate oppression operate at the macro and micro levels. Macro level includes the cultural and social relations and structures that generate oppression, including the larger "forces in society, such as capitalism; governments and their economic, social, financial, and international policies; religious and cultural institutions and international trade and financial bodies" (Baines, 2011, p.4). The micro level social relations or personal level illustrated below, "include social norms, every day practices, workplace-specific policies and processes, values, identities, and so-called common sense" (Baines, 2011, pp. 4-5). The following diagram, originally proposed by Baines (2011), shows the various realms of oppression.

### Realms of Oppression

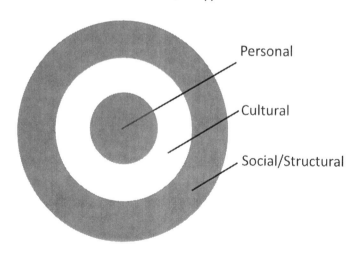

*Source*: Baines (2011).

One student wrote this about her experiences in Finland that illustrates this picture:

> I have worked in homes where youth face many problems. I have not seen any workers or professionals place the blame on the individual or their parents. The workers strive to see the history of the problem, the social environment of the children and their parents, and the way that these problems are placed on children by society. The individuals are experiencing these problems first hand, yet they are taught that there are a number of different societal factors that may help to form the issue at hand. The goal of the organization is to identify these societal factors that are influencing the youth, and abolish them altogether leading to a more functional life for these youngsters.

In the next illustration, Dominelli (1988) shows the three planes on which racism operates, and the ways that social relations lead to oppression interact at

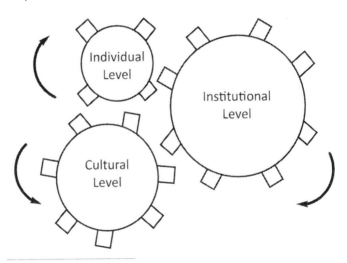

*Source*: Dominelli (1988).

the micro and macro levels. At the individual or micro level, personal attitudes which negatively evaluate or pre-judge marginalized peoples including behaviours based on attitudes which discriminate against marginalized peoples, influence and are influenced by social reactions at the cultural level. This includes values, beliefs or ideologies which affirm the superiority of one group of people. This is influenced by, and influences social relations, at the institutional level and includes all policies, procedures, laws, practices, and outputs of an organization. The outcome is the unequal treatment of marginalized peoples.

One student wrote about structural oppression after reflecting on her international exchange with immigrants and refugees:

> Conversations of class, race, and inequality are hot topics at my placement, especially at lunch time around the kitchen table. Racism is something refugees have to deal with all the time. For example many Africans cannot find apartments because the land lords do not accept black people. Resumes in Belgium are required to have a photo of the applicant. I explained that in other countries it is not required to include a photo or even a full name, just the first initial because an employer can identify the applicant's culture, race, gender or religion. Attaching a photo can identify a person's age, race, gender, which can create inequality of opportunity. They acknowledged what I was saying and could see how it could create inequality.

## 2. Experiences shaped by multiple oppressions

The second theme addresses multiple oppressions. People experience oppressions due to their gender, class, disability, sexual orientation, age, race, ethnicity, and religion. Many people embody more than one status that compounds each other. While doing an internship in Europe, for example, with migrants it is important to be cognisant of the multiple oppressions that they experience due to being migrants, possibly from a group of people who are seen as undesirable like "gypsies," women, and people of colour. These oppressions reinforce each other to further disenfranchise migrants from society.

One student touches on intersecting oppressions in her discussion of the treatment of young migrants:

> Unaccompanied minors typically leave their country due to problems within the family, poor economic and social conditions in their country of origin, and a general lack of opportunity. Due to the risks involved in illegally crossing borders, as well as prevailing gender norms and expectations, an overwhelming majority of these youth are male. Third country agreements within Europe mean that whatever country the migrant applies for is where he or she must reside until the process is completed. So, for instance, if a person first goes to Italy and applies for asylum, and then decides to move to Austria in search of a better social, environmental or economic situation, once discovered by Austrian officials, the person will be ordered back to Italy. In Austria, every resident (including temporary residents like myself) must register their residency with their city. The police then have the authority to conduct random checks for resident permits. As a white female, I have never been asked to produce this identification, however ethnic minority males are asked to produce proof of residence on a regular basis. So asylum seekers who are not authorized to be living in the country are regularly caught and detained by the police, and forced to leave the country. While the asylum process is in progress, these young migrants are, in effect, completely immobile.

## 3. Participatory approaches

The third theme of integrating participatory approaches is important in the human services because it reminds us that we can learn from other people's rich histories and strengths. When doing an international exchange it is important to be mindful of that history as well as indigenous practices and customs. It is important to not impose your own ideas of what practice should look like but to allow people to help us learn how to adapt our usual ways of working with their indigenous practices. The following is one student's thoughts about an experience in Australia:

The Australian views of the Aboriginal peoples here has probably been one of the most interesting and obvious differences that I have experienced so far, as well as one of the most exciting.... I was here for "Sorry Day" (we watched it in the lecture hall through a projector), which was pretty exciting and monumental in Australian history, as the government, both the prime minister and the leader of the opposition actually said the words "I'm sorry", along with quite significant speeches. The leader of the opposition also mucked things up for himself with a few other statements he made, but that's beyond the point. The apology was given for the members of the Stolen Generation, which are basically the equivalent of the First Nations children who were relocated to residential schools in Canada. ...It seems so silly that we hold on to those words. Why not apologize? Really, it was a terrible, terrible thing that was done to the people that were here first and there is no reason not to be sorry for it occurring.

## 4. Self-reflective practice

Lastly, we cannot understate the importance of self-reflective practice and on-going social analysis, especially in international exchanges. In order to analyze our own positions as oppressor and possibly as oppressed we must engage in self reflection. The following are three examples of oppressive situations that students encountered during their exchange.

### Student 1

I was unable to name it until my friend, who is an immigrant and a woman of colour, shared two incidences with me. One was the experience of being spat on by a white male, and the other was being treated courteously by her white co-workers but never being invited to social gatherings. For her, the second incident was more hurtful, she felt invisible and silenced. She could not point her fingers on the act: it was so trivial and mundane, but constant. The impact was very strong, stronger than being spat on. The invisibility and unconscious nature of such acts make it hard for those on the outside to understand. In turn, it makes it hard for those suffering from them to voice out their experiences without being trivialized or denied.

### Student 2

A woman of colour who was involved in an international exchange in Austria commented that she was one of very few people of colour in the small town where she was participating in an exchange. When she would ride the bus older men would openly stare at her. One even asked if

*continued...*

> he could touch her hair. She was frightened by this experience as she had never been such a visible minority in other cities where she had lived. She chose to sit closer to the driver and not make eye contact with people on the bus.

It is up to you to decide how to deal with these uncomfortable situations where it feels like you are being treated like an object and nothing more. In the second example, the students could take on an educational role. Maybe the host country has few people of colour and instead of being offended by the gesture, the student could take the opportunity to educate people and talk to them.

### Student 3

Young Moroccan men suffer many injustices from the government, the public, and especially from the police. A couple weeks ago, I went with my supervisor to visit a Moroccan client in prison. This boy was approximately 16-years-old. He had been to Bologna for Ramadan, and on his way home, police found a large quantity of drugs somewhere on the train. As the only Moroccan man on the train he was arrested for drug trafficking, despite the fact that the drugs were not on his person and there seemed to be little evidence connecting him to it. This boy was imprisoned for about four months, and claimed that he was innocent. My supervisor heard from a number of boys in the community that he was not guilty. A couple weeks before our visit, this client got extremely desperate and depressed about his situation and cut himself all over his arms, legs, and stomach. As a punishment for this self-harm, the prison officials moved him into the adult section of the jail, where he now remains.

# Anti-Oppressive Practice and the International Experience

As a student preparing to go to a different country, there are educational tools and exercises that can be completed to help understand why people might treat you the way they do or why you might experience situations differently than local people.

1.  You should do an analysis of the history of their host county in relation to domination, colonization, and exploitation. How does this history relate to your own country of origin? What does your particular ethnic, age, gender, sexual orientation status look like from the perspective of the local people in the host country?

2.  An excellent preparation for working and living anti-oppressively is to challenge your own social location. What does it mean to look at your social location?

> Social location refers to a person's affiliation or categorization within webs of oppression and privilege. Strands of the webs include race, age, gender, sexual orientation, class, religion, and so forth. People are shaped, but not determined, by their social location. That is, individuals have the capacity to make change and to understand the world independently of the storylines provided to them by society. While people are influenced by their social location, the sum total of who they are, and what they choose to do within this is always changing and offers huge potential for personal and social transformation. (Baines, 2007, p. 24)

The following case example of social location by one of the author's who lived in Ghana for two years helps to clarify the concept.

When I went to Ghana, I knew little about colonization. One of my reasons for going to Africa to volunteer was because I felt uncomfortable around black Africans and was racist towards them in the United States and Britain. I felt going to Ghana would help me in overcoming this racism. Ghana was a British colony and was one of the first country's to become independent. I was a volunteer teaching social work at the University of Ghana, Legon. My first encounter with my own racism was being uncomfortable with my boss, an extremely intelligent black African woman. Where did that feeling come from? Why was I uncomfortable with a black boss? My second experience was realizing that although there were few white people in Ghana, I was still a privileged minority due to the colonizers socialization concerning colour and white superiority. Still today, a whiter shade of black is seen as better than a darker shade of black. My privilege came from being white and British and I benefited from this. It took me a good year of living in Ghana to see beyond colour, seeing these people as human beings just like me, no better and no worse.

While we understand that not all students who engage in an international exchange are white or male or people of colour, we hope that these examples can be helpful to all students in their process of self reflection. Peggy McIntosh, Associate Director of Wellesley College Centre for Research on Women, unpacks her own experience of the duality of oppression and being an oppressor. Follow this URL to see her essay "White Privilege: Unpacking the Invisible Backpack": www.amptoons.com/blog/files/mcintosh.html.

The following is an exercise that can be completed in order to understand the concepts of social location and how an anti-oppressive perspective can have an impact on a student's exchange.

*Exercise one:*

This exercise involves an examination of your own experiences. How would you define who you are? What privileges, challenges, and oppressions have you experienced in your life?

## Wheel of Oppression

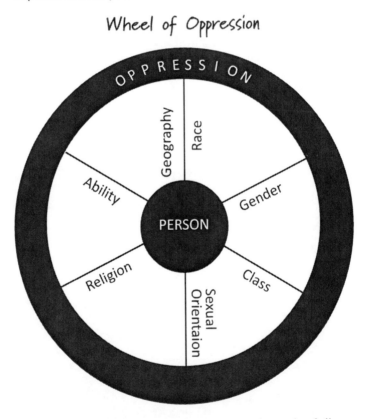

The first step is for students to draw the following model in their journal. This is a revised version of a model McIntosh (2006) refers to as the **Wheel of Oppression**. We added geography to the wheel to account for one's country of origin or where one is currently living. Based on what you have read so far in this chapter, go back to the circle and fill in each area with your own privileges and oppressions. You may want to share your wheel and any thoughts about your own privileges and oppressions with a friend, another student also engaging in an international exchange or your academic Sherpa.

Once you are in the host country re-examine the circle and reflect on the following questions:

1. How do my privileges interact/relate/connect to the people in my host country? How do they see me in relation to my privileges?

2. How do my oppressions interact, relate or connect to the people in my host country? Do they see me as being oppressed? How do they see me in relation to my oppression? If you feel comfortable share this with others.

Many international exchanges are uni-directional in terms of who benefits from the experience. At times the local people in the host country benefit less and are left picking up the pieces of a student who was not conscious of their actions. Anti-oppressive perspective sees the importance of reciprocity as an important part of any exchange.

## Exercise two:

It is important to be open and creative in thinking about what it means to be useful in your host country. What they consider to be useful can be very different. The attitude that you bring to making a contribution is also important. Go through the following questions and write short answers to them.

1. In past field placements or other volunteer experiences how did you know that you were being useful, helping others or making a contribution? Did you rely on evaluations of your performance by others? Did you rely on the facial expressions of the people you worked with?

2. Based on the previous exercises on self awareness and the learning that you have gained

about your host country how might you predict
the ways that you will be helpful?

3. How can you support yourself to be open and
   flexible in your thinking about what is helpful in
   your host country?

4. Revisit what you have written concerning your
   assumptions a month into your field placements
   and see what has changed.

It is easier to be negative about particular
people or cultures when there is no involvement in that
culture. Objectifying a people's way of life gives us the
privilege to criticize it. Once a student has friends from
that culture and gets used to the culture, then understanding can be gained to explain some of the differences and similarities between cultures and less
criticism occurs. However, for many students, it is very
easy to stay within the environments provided by their
own country, as well as other students, particularly if
they do not know the language. By meeting and engaging with local people, a greater awareness of one's own
responsibility of practicing anti-oppressively will take
place.

## Conclusion

The most important attitudes to take to any
international exchange are humility and a non-judgmen-
tal attitude. Going to a host country with an open mind
and an open attitude to reciprocity can make or break
an internship. Understanding your own social location
before going abroad will help to prepare for the unexpected challenges of racism and oppression that may be
experienced or that others will experience by you. We
are both the oppressor and the oppressed and understanding these possible actions will help students act in
a more anti-oppressive way.

Finally, one student wrote a critical analysis of a
test that has been used to determine the age of unac-
companied minors in Belgium. She looked at the cultural

and institutional facets of oppression that come into play in this test.

## Critical reflection journal entry: Age test

When young people arrive in Belgium without a recognized adult accompanying them, the police or other border control body is obliged to ask their age and accept their answer at face value temporarily regardless of appearances. If they say they are less than 18-years-old, they are considered a mineur étranger non-accompagné (MENA) [non-accompanied foreign minor]. They are then transferred to an orientation and observation centre for MENA like NOH until a more long-term solution is found where they can await the processing of their application.

When a young person first comes into contact with a Belgian institution without sufficient documentation, the Service des tutelles (Guardianship Service) and the Office des Étrangers (Foreigner's Office) are notified. Many young people present themselves as minors to the Belge authorities for a number of important reasons. The most prominent of which is to avoid being sent to a closed centre. Closed centres are detention institutions for adults who are found to be in Belgium illegally. In Belgium it is illegal to send an individual without legal documentation younger than 18 to a closed centre unless the child is deemed so young that to live in a reception centre separated from his or her parent(s) would be more damaging than living in a detention centre (La détention des mineurs). An individual can be sent to a closed centre for a variety of reasons such as: arriving at a border without legal documentation to enter the territory; a pre-

*continued...*

vious refugee application in another state of the European Union; those who are considered to pose a danger due to the nature in which they came into contact with Belge authorities, for instance, committing a crime that involved violence or the threat of violence, or the illegal transfer of individuals into the territory (human trafficking) (Guide on the Asylum Procedure in Belgium). A closed centre is typically referred to as a detention centre, and is essentially run as a prison for illegal immigrants, refugees, and other displaced persons. There is significantly more freedom and autonomy in an open centre. It is often in the best interest of the young person to declare that they are a minor if there is any risk that as an adult they could be sent to a closed centre or deported immediately.

If a minor is applying for asylum as a refugee or applying for residency papers, they receive a lawyer and a legal guardian to help them navigate the system and the procedure. They are also enrolled in school as soon as possible which is a big draw for many young people who either have never had the opportunity to attend school, or who had to leave school for the same reasons that they fled their country of origin.

After meeting with the young person there is the opportunity for an employee of Service des tutelles to signal a doubt of proclaimed age (Sur les méthodes de détermination de l'âge à des fins juridiques). This is where the age test comes into play. The age test is a medical assessment to determine the approximate age of a young person. It was developed by Greulich and Pyle in 1959. The test is based on comparing the physical measurements of the young person in question, to either an atlas of measurements

*continued...*

taken by Greulich and Pyle of a Caucasian-American population in the 1950s, or to an atlas of similar statistics by Tanner and Whitehouse (1959; 1962) from a middle-class British population from an even earlier time period (Sur les méthodes de détermination de l'âge à des fins juridiques). Most young people who are sent for the age determination are examined in three basic ways: the left wrist, the clavicle, and dental x-rays (Sur les méthodes de détermination de l'âge à des fins juridiques). Each of these three components are apparently compared to the atlas of statistics thus rendering three separate (and often not the same) ages. These three age results are then averaged and this number becomes the official age determination of the young person.

There are a number of problems with the assessment from a structural perspective. It has been very difficult to locate information critically analyzing the accuracy of the test on either medical or ethical grounds so some of the criticism that follows is purely speculative on my part. The test was developed on a Caucasian, middle class American and British population in the 1950s (Sur les méthodes de détermination de l'âge à des fins juridiques). It is currently in practice for primarily an African, Arabic, and Eastern European population. These two groups differ in a number of ways, which could potentially influence the accuracy of the results. It was designed for use on a genetically different population, there are potentially physical differences between individuals bone composition, skeletal frame, and body structure between the testing population and the current population of practice. For people who have fled their country of origin, it is not uncommon to have participated in strenuous physical labour

*continued...*

since a young age. This work naturally changes the body's composition and physique from a young person who has spent most of their days sitting at a desk in school. There is also a difference in the financial ability, knowledge, and resources to achieve and maintain dental hygiene to the same standards as the testing population. If one has not been educated in terms of dental hygiene; does not have the financial resources to buy toothbrushes, toothpaste, and floss; has not ever had the opportunity to visit a dentist; or does not have regular or reliable access to something as simple as water to facilitate oral hygiene this must impact the state of the dental structure. It is logical to think that teeth which have been neglected by western standards would appear older. The quality and quantity of an individual's diet affects that person's development of physical, mental, and dental health. Poverty heavily influences the ability to attain and sustain adequate nutrition (UNICEF: Nutrition). In addition, worldwide standards and experience with nutrition has changed dramatically over the last 50 years since the test was developed (Sur les méthodes de détermination de l'âge à des fins juridiques).

In 2006, The National Academy of Medicine in France was asked by the French Minister of Health and Solidarity and the French Minister of Justice to evaluate the effectiveness of the age test for the MENA population particularly for individuals of African, Asian, and Eastern European descent (Chaussain, 2006). The response provided by the National Academy of Medicine states that the test developed by Greulich & Pyle (1959) is effective for determining with relative precision within six months for youth younger than 15 years of age, however cannot reliably distinguish

continued...

between individuals between the ages of 16 and 18, and there is even less certainty after the age of 18 (Chaussain, 2006; Sur les méthodes de détermination de l'âge à des fins juridiques). It is thus not only unfortunate that the test in practice is used almost exclusively on asylum seekers over the age of 16 to determine if they will legally be declared minors or not, but medically and ethically unsound. In response to questions around race, the academy states that no racial differences have been demonstrated to date (Chaussain, 2006). It does not explain whether no racial differences have been found because after thorough research and investigation there were statistically significant results or because differences have not been studied or researched in this context at all. This is certainly an important distinction.

In practical terms, it seems to be widely understood by social services agencies and workers that the test is unjust. One worker I spoke to described the test's ability to accurately predict a young person's age like throwing a dart at a target blindfolded. I have also heard much anticdotal evidence to suggest that the test is not applied indiscriminately across ethnic identities. The signalling of "doubt of declared age" is made for all MENA by a single person at Service des tutelles (Plateforme Mineurs en exile). The results of the test can significantly influence the course of a young person's application given that children are necessarily afforded more protection due to their increased vulnerability (Sur les méthodes de détermination de l'âge) Although Service des tutelles can take into consideration the advice or information provided to them by any of the participating partner agencies, unless they have a verified document declaring the identity and age

*continued...*

of the young person, it is still one person who decides whether or not a young person will be sent for the age test. It is a much more subjective process than I would feel comfortable with as a young asylum seeker.

Due to the conditions under which many young people flee their country of origin, most do not arrive with passports and birth certificates. It can seriously jeopardize the success of their asylum application if they attempt to procure their identity documents. If a person is able to contact the government or administrative bureau of their country of origin, the Belge government can decide that the individual does not have any fear of prosecution from the government, its police or military forces, and that they can sufficiently be protected by other individuals or factions by said government (Guide on the Asylum Procedure in Belgium). It is a very precarious position to be in, especially for a legitimate minor: arrive without documentation and risk being deemed an adult by the age test, possibly being detained or deported, or attempt to procure identity documentation and risk being deported. I have not yet discovered any community action coalitions or other organizations that are publicly opposing or taking action against the social injustice of the test. I would very much like to learn more about this aspect and how the process can move forward in an ethical way given the fact that so many young people without legal documentation to be in Belgium declare themselves to be minors. It would likely necessitate major changes at all levels of jurisdiction. I think the obvious complications and guaranteed problems that would arise in changing the system would not outweigh the advances in social justice for the asylum seekers.

*continued...*

# Reflection Questions

1. Which of these exercises do you feel changed your way of thinking about your international exchanges?
2. What was your reaction to reading Peggy McIntosh's essay on White Privilege: Unpacking the Invisible Backpack?
3. What do you anticipate will be the challenges that you will face in relation to oppression and privilege?
4. How you will make a contribution in the country that you will travel to?

# Chapter 2

## Starting the Process

Since you are exploring the idea of completing an exchange outside your home country, there are some basic questions you should consider before moving forward. In the following chapter we will address some of the most salient questions and issues to guide you in making the decision to engage in an international exchange. The format is easy to use. Each element will in turn be expanded to give you more ideas on how to proceed.

## Does Your School Offer International Experiences?

If you are interested in doing an international exchange you need to find out if your school offers this program. You can contact the designated person in charge of exchanges, whom we are calling your academic Sherpa, or the international office of your school.

If your school does not offer international exchanges, you may be motivated to make the case that there is a growing trend, not only to "internationalize" social work and human services, but to encourage exchanges abroad. A list of references to aide you in making this case are included at the end of the book.

On the next page there is a worksheet that you can photocopy to help you prepare for your international exchange. Following the worksheet we present other questions and ideas to help you think through your answers to these questions.

## Worksheet
## Preparing For Your International Exchange:

Answer these questions

- ☐ Does your school already offer international exchanges?
- ☐ Does your institution support it? What does that support look like?
- ☐ How does your school promote/advertise international exchanges? How will you find out about what already exists?
- ☐ What is the application process? What are the assessment criteria that will be used to decide if you will be accepted? Some of these might include: ability to handle stress and problem solve, maturity, academic ability, references from previous exchanges, ability to access resources, emotional intelligence.
- ☐ What can you expect from your relationship with the faculty member responsible for the exchange?
- ☐ Does your school have a roster of organizations willing to engage in an international exchange or do you have to find such an organization yourself? What support does your school provide in this process?
- ☐ Are there other required educational components of the exchange? For example, attending a seminar, attending language classes; writing a paper, participating in regular skype sessions, contributing to weekly blogs related to the exchange experience?
- ☐ Is there financial support available for you to pay for the flight, living expenses in a foreign country, medical coverage, insurance, and other expenses?
- ☐ Does your school provide support in finding housing in another country?
- ☐ Does your school provide support in obtaining a visa, if necessary, and registering in a foreign institution?

# Does Your Institution Support International Exchanges? What Does That Support Look Like?

Is internationalization important for your institution? Do they have an international policy? Do they have an international office? This information can usually be found on the university's web page under International. Many universities list the support they give to outgoing students. This may include information on available grants, the application process and deadlines; defining procedures and restrictions for applying for permission to enrol in an international field experience;

---

*One program's web site description of exchange process:*

Exchanges involve unpaid or volunteer work at a chosen organization. While exchanges do not involve taking academic courses, they may include written assignments and credits may be earned.

Students normally begin preparation for the exchange at the end of their second year. The process typically begins with a workshop in early April to introduce students to writing CVs and cover letters and the process of searching for an exchange.

Students are then responsible for contacting potential host organizations and securing an exchange placement. While final decisions for exchange placement remain with the host organization, the Undergraduate Supervisor will support students in this process by providing feedback on draft resumes, cover letters, and by writing letters of introduction to potential host organizations, as necessary.

---

*Source:* Accessed August 15, 2012 from http://www1.carleton.ca/polisci/current-students/study-abroad-programs/

and a list of inter-university agreements with universities in different parts of the world that may facilitate student exchanges.

## How Does Your School Promote International Exchanges? How Will You Find Out About What Already Exists?

The international office, if your institution has one, would advertise international exchanges. They may have a brochure that lists specific international options. They may also include this information on their web site. Your specific department may have an international committee or person, academic Sherpa, designated as the contact person who holds the responsibility of advertising international exchanges. Many of the skills that you would use in a job search can be employed in finding an exchange. You need to think about your interests, skills, and previous experiences in deciding what kind of exchange would best suit your needs, and what kind of organization would fit your learning style. You need to produce a resume that highlights the experiences that would make you attractive to an organization in the field in which you are interested.

One school's criteria for eligibility are generally based on consideration of the following issues:

- maturity of student and demonstrated ability to follow-through
- high level of self-direction, initiative, clarity of purpose
- good level of academic performance (we will obtain a transcript)
- strength of proposal
- quality of student's references
- strong placement evaluation if the student has done a previous placement

*continued...*

- appropriate rationale for placement
- why learning needs could be better met at a distance than locally
- consideration of financial needs of student /financial issues related to placement
- consideration of a student's future employment possibilities

*The same school's requirement for a proposal requesting permission to be involved in an international placement*

*Student proposal*

Students must develop an exchange proposal

**Part I** (submitted five months in advance of the placement)

In this section of the proposal students should address the following:

1. why the student wishes to do an international placement
2. what are the student's learning objectives
3. where is the student wanting to go and why
4. the names of two faculty who would be prepared to provide a verbal reference

*Also submit a current resume*

**Part II** (submitted three months in advance)

In this section students should provide the following:

5. an outline of a possible exchanges, detailing the learning opportunities and how a specific exchange will meet the student's learning objectives

*continued...*

6. additional information about the setting(s) that will help the coordinator understand the learning opportunity
7. who would supervise the student and her/his credentials (preferably his/her resume)
8. draft learning objectives
9. suggestions for how the placement seminar requirement might be met if an on-line chat seminar is not available
10. while the coordinator is responsible for assigning a faculty liaison, identify any suggestions of who might be available to act as faculty liaison (consider schools of social work in the community)

**Part III** (submitted two months in advance)

11. identify what cultural / international orientation the student will participate in prior to departure in order to prepare for the cultural differences and who will provide this orientation. (The International Student Services Office provides a one-day orientation in early April each year).
12. address the issue of reciprocity given possible language limitations, the historical context of social work in that country, and how to make a contribution in a culturally meaningful manner
13. address how the student will finance this experience. The School does not have the institutional means to help students finance an international placement. It is the responsibility of the student to explore financial options
14. provide a risk assessment (safety concerns) of the environment where the student will be working

*continued...*

15. address how the student will present an aspect of his/her experience to the School or community, if feasible
16. address health and insurance coverage
17. sign an Assumption of Risks, Responsibility and Liability Waiver

*Source:* Wiebe (2011). Retrieved from http://www1.carleton.ca/socialwork/ccms/wp-content/ccms-files/BSW-MSW_Distant-Guide-lines_2012W.pdf

# What Can You Expect From Your Relationship With Your Academic Sherpa?

It is important to identify if there is one person responsible for the exchange process. You need to clarify with that individual how often you will have contact with each other while planning the exchanges as well as once you are abroad. Will email communication or skyping suffice or do you need to meet in person? You need to clarify any assignment requirements and departmental expectations. The next chapter will discuss this important relationship in more detail.

# Does Your School Have A Roster Of Organizations Willing To Engage In An International Exchange Or Do You Have To Find An Organization To Work In Yourself?

If you have to find one yourself, what support does your school provide? What support will the organization provide in helping you get settled in your new city?

Some faculty members, including your academic Sherpa, may have personal relationships that they have developed over their careers that will be helpful to you.

They may also have formal ties in the form of a MOU, Memorandum of Understanding, related to international exchanges. It is important to talk to a number of faculty members aside from your academic Sherpa for ideas about exchange opportunities because they may have contacts that could be potentially useful. There are many questions that you need to ask to clarify what kinds of supports the organization may or may not provide for you. One student wrote:

> The staff and advisors at the Finnish social service organization have been extremely kind and helpful to my Canadian colleagues and me. From finding us an apartment, to picking us up from the train station and lending us bikes and cell phones, we have had a firsthand experience at the Finnish way of hospitality. This important aspect of the culture can help explain the extreme care and passion that the government has for its citizens, and why Finland is one of the most socially progressive countries in the world. In Finland, the needs of the people come first and foremost. To me, this is how every country in the world should be. By keeping the well being of all citizens in mind, no matter age, social or financial background, societies can become places of higher equality and form a stronger social cohesion. From what I have learned, experienced, and seen so far, this is one of Finland's main goals.

## What Are The Other Educational Components Of The Exchange?

*Are you required to attend a seminar, language classes; write a paper, regular Skype sessions, weekly blogs related to exchange?*

In later chapters we offer some examples of different assignments that you may be required to complete. It is important to clarify assignment expectations before you agree to participate in an international exchange to make certain that you will have access to the necessary computer and internet technology, and that you have the interest in completing these kinds of assignments.

## What Financial Support Is There For You?

Do you have access to institutional funding such as bursaries? Do you know where to look for this information? Do you know the deadlines? Do you know the cost of living where you plan on doing your placement? Do you know if there are costs for such things as visas? Medical examinations? Vaccinations? How will you pay for those costs?

## What Support Does Your School Provide In Finding Housing In Another Country?

Do you have any contacts to help you in your search for housing? Are there people in your department who can help with housing? Can you access the contact information (i.e., email address and facebook) for any students who have previously engaged in similar international exchanges? Is there a housing registry on the web site of a university in the city where you hope to live or on the city's website? One student wrote about the support that she received:

> I would recommend that the students from the previous year act as "tutors" or "mentors" for the current exchange students. In Austria, I had M (last year's exchange student) helping me to secure housing, picking me up at the airport, showing me around the town, explaining to me what my German lease says, and communicating with my landlord who spoke no English. I feel strongly that without his help, I would have been extremely lost

*continued...*

in my first few weeks in Innsbruck. He did this voluntarily, and I intend to do the same for the student that comes from Austria next semester; however I would recommend that this become part of the contract to ensure that it happens every year for every student.

## What Support Does Your School Provide In Obtaining A Visa, If Necessary, And Registering In A Foreign Institution?

Most universities will require students to have additional medical insurance for international travel, which can be acquired through private insurance companies. Your academic Sherpa should be able to help you with bureaucratic issues like work permits and police checks. It is important to gain an understanding of the differences between provincial Canadian regulations for these issues as well as the differences between international regulations.

Once you have addressed the questions above it is time to think about what is motivating you to engage in an international exchange. While you are considering the following exercise think back on the issues raised in the previous chapters of the impact of globalization, anti-oppressive practices, and how you will make a contribution during your exchange.

## Integrative Learning Activity: Motivation for Undertaking an International Exchange

Write a short essay (200 words) about what motivates you to complete your placement in an international setting. Share and discuss this essay in a small group of two or three students either face-to-face or online. Reflect on your motivation and those of other students in your group. Some suggested areas of conversation include the following four areas:

1. If one motivation is fascination with other cultures, what was the source of this fascination?

2. If you are motivated by "liking people from another country," consider how historical inequities between your home country and your host country may shape the feelings of citizens of your host country towards you. Therefore, before embarking you would be wise to examine the historical and current relations between your home and host country.

3. The motivation of "liking" also assumes homogeneity of the citizens of the host country. Consider what your reaction might be, if someone from another culture considered you to be like all others from your country. Possibly, their assumption of homogeneity may lead you to feel confused, even outraged, and to inwardly cry out, "Don't judge me by the actions of my fellow citizens or my government. I am an individual!" You, like citizens of your host country, wish to be seen as an individual and not like everyone else from your country.

4. Some students' motivation for an international exchange is to reconnect with their cultural heritage. The following narrative was written by a Canadian-born student whose ancestors were from India. She was completing her exchange in an Indian child-serving organization.

> While I was reading one of the children's files, I came upon the part of the form that said "Caste" and I found myself staring at the word to make sure it was actually there, because I thought the caste system had been abolished in India. I wanted to discuss the issue of caste and its role in Indian society with my supervisor but felt restrained by many factors. First, I was talking as an outsider and didn't want to criticize the social structures too
>
> *continued...*

much. I wasn't well versed on the topic. Secondly, and most important, was the fact that I was talking to a male supervisor. In Canada, this would have made absolutely no difference to me, but for some reason, here in India I think that because I am somewhat familiar with the culture, I'm expected to follow the Indian norms more closely that some of the other students whose families did not immigrate from India. Although my supervisor is very professional and I'm sure considers us equals, for some reason I found myself watching what I say and how I say it. Because of out of respect for him and being mindful of the fact that not only was he my supervisor, but he was male. In my future interactions with him, I want to try and be less worried about the expectations of others being different for me because they know I'm familiar with the language and culture. Hopefully, I can feel free to express myself (within limits) as I would with a supervisor in Canada and not be so conscious of trying to fit into the "Indian way" of doing things.

## Conclusion

Seeing a long list of tasks to be undertaken to begin your exchange may seem daunting. But your exchange will proceed much more smoothly if the proper preparation is accomplished. If you are to trek to the top of high mountains you need to have the appropriate foods, medicines, and safety equipment in your backpack. Even knowing what are appropriate foods, medicines, and safety equipment requires research. The steps listed in this chapter guide this research so that your trek towards your exchange will be successful.

# Reflection Questions

1. Which of the tasks listed above am I most nervous or unsure about?
2. What can I do to make the task less onerous or intimidating?
3. In which of the tasks do I anticipate the most road-blocks?
4. Which task will take the most time to accomplish?
5. Should I prioritize the tasks according to which will take the most time (question 3) or which one I am most anxious about (question 1)?
6. How am I going to address institutional barriers? Am I fully aware of institutional barriers?
7. Have I explored the options for support sufficiently? What have I done to explore the options?

# Chapter 3

## Academic Sherpa's Role

While the trekkers in Nepal often have only one Sherpa guiding their journey, you may be lucky enough to find a number of Sherpas to help you. One of your own personal Sherpas is the person that you will work with to coordinate your international exchange. They may be one of your professors, a field placement coordinator, or someone in the international exchange office at your university. We call this person from the university your academic Sherpa. This person may have a very active role in helping you plan and prepare for your international experience or may lay the ground work and leave the primary responsibility to you to do the leg work. Either way they play an important role and it is imperative that you understand that role. You may encounter Sherpas in the organization where you conduct your exchange and we call them agency Sherpas.

The academic Sherpa has to interact with numerous stakeholders, sometimes simultaneously. One primary stakeholder is the university, which includes the administrative personnel charged with negotiating a Memorandum of Understanding (MOU); international office; scholarship office; and the professor's department, including colleagues and students. Other stakeholders include the funding body; partner universities; foreign embassies; the field agency, if the international exchange includes a field placement component; and lastly, the broader community in which the student will live. This chapter will discuss the various roles that your academic Sherpa may assume while interacting with the various stakeholders.

## Figure 1
## Stakeholder Interactions

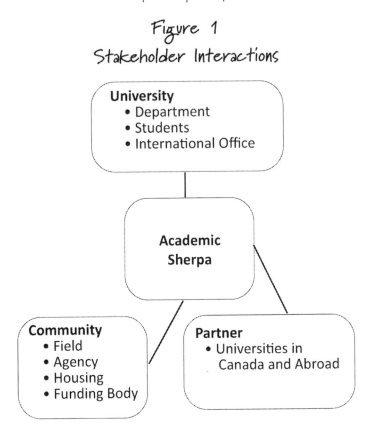

Before we discuss the roles of your academic Sherpa, we will set the stage by discussing responsibilities and the context for thinking about the roles.

## Context

It is important to consider the context within which the academic Sherpa makes decisions and carries out their role. This may remind you of what was discussed in the first chapter about anti-oppressive practice. The Canadian Association of Social Work Education recommends these principals when considering international exchanges:

*Mission and objectives of International Affairs Committee (CASWE):*

The mission of the International Affairs Committee is to encourage and facilitate discussion of issues concerning international collaboration and exchanges and related curricula between social work educators and programs. Our nine principles and objectives include:

1.  examining the systemic and historical contexts of international social work such as colonialism, imperialism, racism, classism, globalization and corporatization, both in the larger society, and within the social work profession;
2.  supporting indigenous knowledge, and encourage discussion of how language plays a role in producing diverse meanings of concepts such as helping, culture, and spirituality;
3.  examining the issue of reciprocity, and promote an expanded discourse among schools of social work regarding its importance and centrality in international social work;
4.  reflecting on the process of how multiple agendas of international exchanges are negotiated between social work educators;
5.  building relationships and a social work presence in the international development field;
6.  promoting curriculum development in relation to international issues in Canadian schools of social work;
7.  promoting the development of ongoing critical discussions pertaining to international issues within schools of social work;
8.  encouraging sharing of relevant resources, models, contact, and information related to international social work; and
9.  encouraging the development of appropriate policies pertaining to the areas identified above.

This is the lens through which your academic Sherpa may view an international exchange and it influences how they make decisions about the exchange.

# Responsibilities of the International Exchange Academic Sherpa

Your academic Sherpa, in most situations, takes responsibility for the international exchange process and the administration of the exchange. The six specific responsibilities include:

1. initiating recruitment and application process;
2. meeting with students and coordinating the negotiations of all student exchanges;
3. assisting students in identifying goals and learning needs applicable to an international exchange;
4. assisting students in the process of completing their paperwork, including visa applications where applicable, and in receiving financial assistance;
5. providing links between the university department or program, partner programs  and the community; and
6. assisting the students in addressing and resolving any serious conflicts and disputes that may arise during the exchange.

We will address these responsibilities in the following sections.

## Roles

We interface with the faculty, students, agencies and many other professional bodies and we have access to a wealth of professional colleagues in the community with whom we can create alliances and collaborations for education. We enjoy their trust and we earn their credibility through our skillful negotiations in establishing learning sites for students. We can tap into this reservoir of community contacts to create projects, evaluate programs and research critical social issues. (Razack, 2002b, pp. 35-36)

Your academic Sherpa will engage in numerous roles with the various stakeholders. These include negotiator, educator, cultural guide, information conduit, risk manager, problem solver, counselor, diplomat, and administrator. We will address each individually.

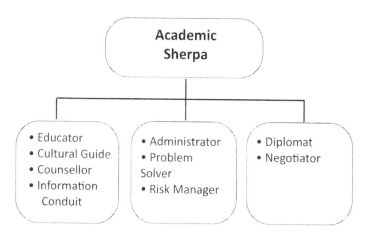

### Risk management

Risk management is activity directed towards the assessing, mitigating, and monitoring of risks. Risks can come from many places and often in ways that you would least expect like accidents, natural causes, and disasters. Risk needs to be managed in a context of anti oppressive values and respect for diversity. It is important for you to understand your institution's risk management protocol as your academic Sherpa will be accountable, for instance, for your safety, ensuring that you receive the necessary vaccinations; and signing your institutions waiver form. Often the International Office of your university will have a waiver form that you will have to complete (see the example at the end of this chapter). Insuring that you will have adequate health and travel insurance is another component of risk management. However, when you are engaging in an exchange in countries where there is conflict like Sierra

Leone or Haïti, you can never completely control for all risks.

The following are two recent examples from our experiences as academic Sherpas. One Canadian social work student, let's call her Paula, who was doing an international field placement in Finland befriended an Indian woman who wanted to bring her home to India. Paula felt that this woman's generosity was an opportunity that she could not refuse. However, Paula did not inform her institution's academic Sherpa prior to leaving for India. They flew from Helsinki to Mumbai. After a wonderful trip to various parts of India and meeting numerous family members, Paula began her return trip to Finland by taking a train to Mumbai. She did not know at the time that a terrorist attack was underway in Mumbai on prominent tourist hotels and the train station. Paula was not aware of the chaos and danger she was entering. Fortunately a concerned Indian woman took Paula under her wing inside the train station and sent Paula immediately to the airport in a taxi rather than to her hotel which was under siege. Paula had to wait a long time to get a flight back to Finland but she was safe until her flight departed. One can never anticipate these kinds of events, but if her academic Sherpa had been informed, Paula would have had an ally to possibly help her get an earlier flight or be informed of what was happening in other parts of the country.

In another incident, Diane, who was going to work with child soldiers in Sierra Leone, refused vaccinations because she believes in naturopathic medicine. After consulting with the university lawyer, a special waiver form was drawn up to exempt the university from liability should Diane contract tropical diseases because she refused vaccination. Diane did return from an amazing learning experience with various forms of malaria and was ill for a number of months. She was not litigious towards the university because she accepted responsibility for her decision. All the relevant stakeholders felt content about having a signed special waiver.

## Information conduit

It is important for students to know what services are offered by the international office at your institution, and your academic Sherpa can inform you of these services. They often offer rides from the airport, social events, trips to local attractions and other cities, and a place to hang out on campus. They may also have information about accommodations. One group of students who were traveling together to engage in an international exchange stayed at the local youth hostel until they were able to find a house that they could rent together. They used contacts at the international office to find a landlord that rented to students.

Academic Sherpas often have travel experience and can assist you with questions, for instance, about negotiating a city, where to get bus passes, how to get a phone card, and how to get access to the university gym. Sherpas will enlist students who have gone on an international exchange and have returned or students who are about to go on an exchange to meet with you to help provide some of this basic information. They are a wonderful resource for you.

## Diplomat

Your academic Sherpa has a history of maintaining relationships with international governmental and non-governmental organizations (NGOs), universities, and community agencies. Nourishing these relationships often requires skills in diplomacy. If, as a student, you require a letter from the host organization or university, and the letter is not sent to you in a timely manner, which delays your travel visa, your academic Sherpa may be required to use their diplomatic skills to gently encourage their international contact to expedite the task.

As international exchanges are resource intensive in terms of the time that your academic Sherpa will need to invest in making preparations, and since universities and other organizations are being asked to do more with fewer resources, your academic Sherpa will need to ensure that he or she has enough time delegated from their department.

## Problem solver

There are many different areas where the academic Sherpa may be called upon to solve problems. In our experience, language fluency is an on-going issue that requires attention. In the following example, when some supervisors of field placements became frustrated with the students' lack of language proficiency, they realized that they needed some creative solutions. The needs of the students for an educational experience has to be balanced with the needs of the organization to have the students engage in meaningful work. Below is a table of solutions generated by one academic Sherpa and two agency Sherpas in the host organizations, one in Poland and one in Austria. We will say more about the importance of language preparation in the next chapter.

---

### Table 1

### 10 Strategies for Supporting Students with Limited Host Language Proficiency

1. Recruit a supportive field instructor who can communicate in the student's language.
2. Secure a placement in a residential social service facility where students can engage more informally with staff and clients such as sharing a meal, participating in field trips, and engaging in recreational activities with the clients.
3. Create opportunities for direct student involvement with younger children who are enthusiastic teachers of their language and eager to have contact with an international social work student.

*continued...*

4. Develop a student learning agreement that requires students to visit a range of community agencies.

5. Integrate field placement tasks that involve shadowing.

6. Pair a visiting student with a local student who is in a same field agency.

7. Recruit field agencies that work in English (for Canadian students) and the language of the host country. For example, several students were placed with NGOs who engaged in macro practices that focused on global issues such as human rights and social justice and related to internationally based organizations.

8. Provide additional support to field instructors by actively consulting on developing an appropriate learning agreement that can accommodate the student's language limitations.

9. Engage field agency colleagues to support the students. For example, one Canadian field instructor developed a weekly rotation for three non-English speaking Polish students that included observation and shadowing of the broad range of programs that were offered by the agency. On a weekly rotation, students were paired with an agency staff member who oversaw their learning objectives. Additionally, the students met individually and in a group for weekly educational supervision with the field instructor who was fluent in Polish.

10. Offer a stipend and a certificate of appreciation to the agency and the field instructor to recognize and reward the additional responsibilities associated with supervising international students.

*Source*: Barlow et al., 2010a.

## Cultural guide

It is important to allow your academic Sherpa to help you understand the host culture. This can be accomplished by preparing yourself as discussed in the previous chapter. Remember that your academic Sherpa has a great deal of travel experience to share. You can never anticipate the kind of cultural misunderstanding or instances or cultural adjustment challenges that will arise. One example that we encountered involved a Canadian student who was not prepared for the difference in culture practices concerning smoking in Austria. He was allergic to cigarette smoke and was not prepared for how prevalent and acceptable smoking is in Europe. This was very difficult for him.

## Counselor

Counseling may take many forms from active listening to your concerns to more traditional counseling which helps you "identify the challenges, obstacles, and problems that interfere with or block achieving your goals, improving your relationships" (Bogo, 2006, p. 63). Your academic Sherpa can be available to provide emotional support if uncomfortable situations occur or to help deal with homesickness. You may also be part of a group of students doing international exchanges who communicate on a regular basis. This may be facilitated by your academic Sherpa. We encountered one student who was robbed at a train station. He felt violated by the experience and became depressed and afraid of leaving his residence.  When he finally contacted his academic Sherpa and told her what happened he was able to express his feelings about the event for the first time. His academic Sherpa helped him become comfortable with the idea of telling other people about his experiences and contacting the police. He was helped to discuss this experience with other students and they provided peer support for him by telling him about their experience of being robbed at home and abroad and how they handled their own feelings. Rather than flee home, which his first instinct, he was able to complete a very successful exchange.

## Negotiator

Negotiating international exchanges requires a great deal of sensitivity and tact. Some of the skills taught in social work practice courses are useful in negotiating, including active listening, showing empathy, and contracting, (van de Sande & Schwartz, 2011).Fisher, Ury, and Patton (1991) developed four steps for principled negotiation:

1. separate the people from the problem
2. focus on interests, not positions
3. generate a variety of possibilities before deciding what to do
4. insist that the results are based on some objective standard.

Your academic Sherpa can be an ally and resource for you when difficulties arise. These difficulties may be minor misunderstandings or serious challenges like in the following example. An international student who was doing an exchange in Canada ran into difficulties at the NGO where he was working as part of his exchange. In his home country he ate with his hands. He knew that this was not socially acceptable in Canada and did not feel proficient enough with western utensils to eat in public, therefore, he would not eat all day. No one at the NGO noticed that he did not eat all day but did notice and commented on the fact that his energy was low, his attention wavered and his production declined as the day wore on. He mentioned this to his academic Sherpa who was able to alert his supervisor in Canada and they brainstormed a solution that would not embarrass the student (Schwartz & van de Sande, 2003).

Another student, a Canadian in Belgium, thought she knew how a women's shelter should be run and felt that the system in Canada was far superior to the one in Belgium. A great deal of

continued...

negotiation went on between her academic Sherpa and her supervisor at the women's shelter because of the student's attitude and the problems that it caused between her and other staff members. You can decide how successful the negotiations were based on what the student wrote in her final evaluation: I did learn something very important about international social work. It is not reasonable to think that you can come into an already established way of working and begin to push against the grain in a determined way. It is more reasonable to first, step back and understand why an agency operates with a certain framework. Once that is achieved, you can then go about making suggestions for change or modification with agency policies and programs. It is an extremely slow process and you must always remember that you are not an expert in this organization or culture, and learning is in reality your main goal.

## Educator

Ultimately your academic Sherpa is an educator. Some of the educational opportunities they provide include pre-departure seminars (examples in appendices), online seminars, discussion sessions for students on whatever computer platform your university uses (i.e., blackboard and WebCt) support for students, and creating other appropriate learning opportunities.

One Canadian university, for example, requires students to take a course prior to their international exchange entitled "International Placement: Self, Identity and Diversity." This is a required course for students who have been accepted for an international placement in the MSW program. The goal of the course is to prepare students for an international learning opportunity and to support the integration of their learning and practice across cultures and settings, including an improved understanding of reciprocal and mutual learning between and among cultures. Cross-cultural learning, colonialism, oppression, and anti-racism are discussed. One student reflected on the course that she took once she had returned from her overseas exchange:

Two years ago, I had taken a social work class on International Community Development. During my field placement in Europe, I reflected back on what I learned in this class. Some of the concepts we discussed that have stayed with me were being open to learn from each other when entering a new culture, actively seeking to exchange ideas, and most importantly, treating the people from the host country as experts in their lives. I really found this to be the key. I believe that even if there are very little resources available, it is important to be sensitive and open to discovering and acknowledging creativity and working with and building on the resources and strengths, which are already present. There is nothing worse than coming to a new environment and having the attitude of having all the answers and best way of practice. This kind of behaviour only discourages collaboration and burns bridges between the hosts and the outside professional.

Coming to the centre where I was doing my field placement, I could have easily slipped into the role of an outsider who comes in and compares and judges everything according to what I am used to and familiar with from back home. Even though I saw how much the centre was lacking when it came to having the support of other community resources (which were almost non-existent) or how unappreciated and overworked the staff seemed to be, I tried very hard not to focus on what was missing; concentrating instead on what was working

*continued...*

well and what new things I could learn from the staff. When I first visited one of Krakow's neighbourhoods, an overwhelming sea of socialist grey concrete buildings with a population of 200,000 residents, the small socio-therapy centre, "U Siemacha," seemed completely small and insignificant to me. However, as I spent more time there, I began to view it as a small shining gem in the community. There are about 150 children a year who are impacted by this centre. Because the attendance is completely voluntary, children choose for how long and how often they want to attend.

Below is an example of a conversation between students as part of a required Blackboard posting. Blackboard is the computer platform that her host university used to manage courses and allow students to discuss their exchange. These students were in a variety of countries doing international exchanges and were asked to discuss a situation that occurred to them that was funny or not so funny in the course of their daily activities.

*One of the students, who was in India with her son, wrote:*

Student 1: I think I stand out. Particularly when I am walking with my son Ken. We don't look like normal Hindu mother and son at all. Many children here in India look at us curiously, most of them sending us welcoming greetings. Some children ask me to give them 5 rupees after the initial friendly greetings. I often don't say anything back, and walk away, but I have felt a little rock landed on my backside more than I care to remember (I'm quite happy that they didn't use big ones). I have heard that the general public here thinks that all foreigners are

*continued...*

richer than them. Thus foreigners tend to become the targets of shopkeepers, rickshaw drivers, and beggars in this country. It may be true, but I don't see myself as particularly wealthy (not in terms of material goods, however, I consider myself rich in character). I feel that because I look different from them, they assume that I can afford to give 5 rupees each to all the children who ask for it. Ironically, Ken told me that one of the things he likes about India is the fact we can afford so many things, which we usually cannot in Canada. It goes to show that you can't really read a book by its cover. We might look like we have more than enough, but the truth is that we, Ken and I, according to Canadian standards, live a life which is far from glamorous. When I hear that we truly are better off when it comes to having basic necessities, I feel as if I'm learning about "absolute poor" and "relative poor" all over again.

Response of Student 2: I'm sorry to hear people throwing rocks at you! Very perturbing. One of my pet peeves about traveling to poorer regions is how people openly ask you for money. After studying more indigenous cultures, I began to think that maybe people are forthright in asking for money partly because they come from a more sharing culture, where resources are communal... it is not that they are rude and think all foreigners have endless supplies of funds. But hearing that they throw rocks sounds like bad manners. Perhaps it is just another cultural divide or a racist attitude. It makes me wonder if you said nothing at all, would that minimize the stone throwing or do they throw stones whether you greet them or not?

As an educator your academic Sherpa could help the discussion move deeper by having the students discuss the differences between the concepts of "absolute poverty" and "relative poverty," or how coming from a culture where resources are considered communal shapes attitudes and behaviour.

Your academic Sherpa has probably gone through her or his own process of becoming culturally sensitive. The following are some ways they may demonstrate to you their sensitivity and pass this knowledge to you.

## Building cultural knowledge

1. Academic Sherpas will show genuine curiosity about your cultural background, remembering that cultural knowledge is fluid and changing rather than static.

   Louie (2005) urges us to develop skills and strategies for meta cultural sensitivity, which is "the process of personal growth through which both the teacher and the student can progressively attain more sophisticated awareness, understanding and acceptance of cultural difference" (p.24). Step back from your culture with both a critical and empathic eye and note our very human tendency to react negatively when the culturally unexpected occurs.

2. Academic Sherpas will be open to imparting knowledge of their own culture. Both academic Sherpas and students are carriers of culture.

3. Academic Sherpas will help you consider the question: What is culture?

---

### What is culture?

Ways of life, shared behavior, social institutions, systems of norms, beliefs, values and world views that allow people to locate themselves within the universe and that give meaning to their personal and collective experiences (McKenzie & Morissette, 2003, p. 259).

## Be explicit

4.  Academic Sherpas will be explicit about their academic and field agency culture and remain clear about the core values, beliefs, and expectations of appropriate behavior.

    (a) They offer guidance in terms of workplace rules and norms such as gift-giving and receiving, standards of dress, and hierarchy of communication

    (b) They are explicit about assessment, framework for field instruction, beliefs about the nature of the student and faculty or agency Sherpa relationship.

    (c) They ask about your perspective on teaching method, evaluation, and the student and teacher relationship. Are you more comfortable and familiar with Sherpas "telling" in a teacher-directed, highly structured situation? Do you understand the evaluation criteria? Do you view the Sherpa as an expert, a parental figure; someone who offers clear instructions about conduct and assignments?

## Self reflect

5.  Academic Sherpas will be aware of their cultural stereotypes. They will monitor culturally imperialistic attitudes that can infiltrate concerns about language, academic, or practice skills of international students.

6.  Academic Sherpas will consider their attitude and empathy to cultural differences.

7.  Academic Sherpas will guard against the use of a deficit model, which assumes that some cultures are "less than." Cultural baggage is carried by both Sherpa and student.

## Administrator (Policy developer)

Your academic Sherpa might be responsible for creating the policies, procedures, application processes for international exchanges. The following example is from the field of social work. There is another example in Appendix 3 called "Sample Guidelines for International Placements" if you would like to see another school's policy.

*Sample: Policies and procedures for undergraduate international field placements*

The School of Social Work offers students undertaking the second field placement of the BSW program the opportunity to complete an international field placement.

All field placements are developed and coordinated by the Office of Field Education, and usually involve an arrangement with a post-secondary institution abroad. At an undergraduate level, there is no opportunity to develop field placements in sites other than those designated by the Office of Field Education.

The Office of Field Education is committed to ensuring that students receive a quality learning experience that supports integration of social work theories, ethics, and practice, therefore, an integrative seminar will be offered in a blended learning format. This is a graded course that consists of a 3-day intensive seminar offered one Saturday a month beginning 4 months prior to departure and an online component to be completed while the student is in their field placement. Attendance at the 3-day seminar is compulsory.

Applications must be made to the Director of Field Education (or designate) **no later than April 15 for a placement beginning in September**.

Due to the limited pool of international field agencies, students **cannot be guaranteed** a placement. An ad hoc committee comprised of students and faculty members will review the applications to determine suitability. The decision of the committee is final.

Students are responsible of **all costs incurred** including travel, accommodation, tuition, and field instructor fees (where applicable). Limited financial aid is available from the university Awards Office and the Student Union.

## Sample: Student application

Prepare a written letter and proposal (maximum of four pages) that includes:

- Personal and professional learning while in an international field placement and how an international field placement will enhance the goals;
- Preference of field placement site from the list of pre-arranged settings. The letter will include knowledge of the country, its culture, relevant social work issues, second language spoken, any related international coursework and experience, and reason for selection of a particular setting;
- What do you bring to an international field placement in terms of academic preparation, personal experience, and professional experience?
- How is this field placement related to your long term goals?
- Submit two letters of reference that address suitability for an international field placement.

**Prerequisites**: Enrolment or completion on a training course in the language of your host country and successful completion of the introductory field placement. The application package must include your introductory field placement evaluation.

Minimum GPA is 3.25/4

As part of their administrative role your academic Sherpa is also responsible for negotiating a Memorandum of Understanding (MOU) between your university and the organization that will host you. There is an example of a MOU in Appendix 1. Your academic Sherpa has a lot of responsibilities to juggle. In Appendix 2, we included a timetable that some academic Sherpas follow. This will give you an idea of when it is time to address different tasks that need to be accomplished before you leave. Lastly your academic Sherpa may provide you with a checklist to help you prepare for departure (see Chapter 5).

## Conclusion

Your academic Sherpa will play an important role in your international exchange. We have reviewed their many roles. You may not have to take advantage of all of their areas of expertise, but it is important for you to know what kind of help you can expect. In some situations you may have a number of academic Sherpas helping you with different aspects of your exchange.

## Reflection Questions

1. Do you know your academic Sherpa? If not do you know how to find out who to seek as your academic Sherpa?
2. How can you prepare yourself to be culturally sensitive during your exchange? Which of the suggestions presented in this chapter most resonated with you?
3. What are some important questions related to the information presented in this chapter to ask your academic Sherpa during you first meeting with her or him?

# Chapter 4

## Guided Learning

In this chapter we describe numerous educational activities that can enrich your international exchange. An international exchange is a powerful learning opportunity both personally and professionally. What follows is a student's description of how she was transformed by her international exchange experience.

### A field placement to remember

This field placement challenged me to the core of my being–professionally and ethically. When I set out for India I knew it would not be an easy year for me, many people either praise India or vow never to return. I came to India to challenge myself, to force myself to feel uncomfortable and to learn to face my biases and assumptions about myself and others. When I look back over the experiences of the past three months within this placement, three words come to mind; hatred, acceptance, and peace. It is not to say that these were the only themes of my field placement but they over shadowed my every experience and interaction I have had with this country and my inner self. These concepts/themes occurred in no chronological order but rather have over lapped each other throughout my stay here and will continue to do so until I leave. India is the land of polar opposites, life and death, tenderness and cruelty, beauty and ugliness, love and hate, and so on. Only after living here for the past seven months can I find a balance between the extremes within India and am slowing finding a balance within myself.

*continued...*

Hatred was the first emotion and theme that resonated in me that I found both disturbing and alarming. As a young social worker I stressed a lot over my feelings towards the men of this country. Although, as I have said before, I realize the sexual oppression within Indian society and how men are conditioned a certain way, I still struggle with their behaviour. I had a point in my trip where I could say without a doubt that I hated Indian men and this terrified me. What kind of person had I become, let alone a decent social worker? I had let all the negative experiences taint my view of a whole population and it was bordering on racism. I was afraid of them and deemed all Indian men to be the same. There was a dark period in my travels where every man I had interactions with did something inappropriate to me and I had to force myself to get over the disgust I felt. This feeling grew to the point where I was soon mad and scared of young boys, feeling that they too would do something to me, given the chance. I observed society and realized that my gender oppression was an old story here and that the women are seen as responsible for the sexual outbursts of men. I was told that I was responsible for men grabbing me, harassing me, and masturbating in front me in public. This is what led to my all out, thankfully brief, period of hating the men of India. This was before I arrived in Kerala, the socialist state where women are considered equal.

It was within my field placement where I met and became good friends with several Indian men. I was so ashamed at how I had felt that I confessed to nearly each one about how I thought I would never like Indian men and certainly never have one as a friend. My dark cloud of misunderstanding was lifted and I began to see that my feel-

continued...

ings were a result of fear and that hatred was only perpetuating the cycle of victim and perpetrator. As I began to visit other agencies and conduct home visits I came to see the total uselessness of hatred and how it can paralysis people from doing any real good. I was so wrapped up in my conceived notions that I failed to see the good in Indian men. I met several poor families where the men of the house were generous, kind, and hard working, trying desperately to keep their families out of poverty. Had I still been blinded by hatred I would not have been able to hear their story and offer them support. I was in a dangerous head place that was lifted only when I was able to see the reality of the situation. Today, I can with all honesty, state that I do not hate Indian men. I'm not sure I ever really did, but I do struggle with their society and the few choice actions of a minority within. I saw the blinding power of hatred and now totally refrain from using the word. When one is able to step back from a situation, you can easily see the uselessness of hating and the power of acceptance.

Beyond accepting the men of this country, India has provided me with several ethically challenging scenarios in which I have had to learn the concept of acceptance. The whole caste system has really given my head a good shake. For Indians it is a system of order and semblance that is now a cornerstone of their culture and tradition, whereas for me it's an archaic system used to further divide the rich and the poor. I have learned through many long conversations that I cannot challenge their perception and win, the caste system is too old and has more experience dealing in India than I have. When you are born in a certain caste or out of it, your life is predetermined and you are forced to

*continued...*

accept your fate in hopes of being reborn to something better. There is a certain type of apathy towards the whole thing; people believe they deserve to be within their given societal ranks; hence they must be happy with what they have as it is not going to get any better this time around. For someone with no faith this is a hard concept to swallow let alone accept. I struggled to make sense of their rational for a long time and learned I could not, so I decided I didn't have to. As I walk the streets littered with sleeping, deformed, mangled, and dirty bodies, I still believe they deserve better. I do not have to accept the caste system and what it stands for. What I do have to accept are the views of others and their way of life.

As with the lepers, I have to respect and support their way of living, regardless of whether I believe it is in their best interests. It took me a long time to clearly learn the idea of acceptance. I thought I was a poor social worker because ethically I believed the caste system to be outdated and oppressive and could not accept a huge part of my host country's culture. I felt like I was being too closed minded and judgmental, even though I knew my personal ethics were being challenged. I spent a long time really examining what I believed to be right and realized that being a good social worker is about having strong values, ethics, and morality, and upholding these principles. As with many things I have faced within this field placement, I have learned the difference between being judgmental and biases, versus being true to one's values, is acceptance. Before I came to India I would have said I was very accepting of others, not being fully aware of what acceptance meant. After being quiet for some time now I can say that acceptance is a hard thing to do, and it takes time.

*continued...*

Anyone who has ever lived in India can tell you what a daily struggle, emotionally, mentally, and physically it is to be here. While at home, I led what I thought was a stressful life; full time student, two jobs, a member of a theater group and social butterfly. I heard so much about India and what a peaceful place it was, I assumed that upon getting here I would finally be stress free. Despite being totally overwhelmed 24 hours a day and feeling at times more stressed than I thought humanely possible, India did give me peace. One Indian word for peace is *shanty,* used more often by travelers than locals and used too much. Most people reference places as being *shanty.* India to me is *shanty*, but not necessarily in the typical quite, still and calm way that one would expect. In my field placement I have come to meet a variety people from different religions, cultures, and socio-economic backgrounds, and nearly all of them seem to embody this idea of peace. Peace among each other and within themselves. India is a wonderfully diverse country that has been able to, for the most part, peacefully blend together. People are accepting of others and embrace difference. People still marry inside their religion and caste but the younger generations are slowly changing. On a personal level, most people have an inner calmness about them. Perhaps this is because nearly everyone has a religion to follow or maybe it is because inner peace is a virtue and strength in India. In Canada we pride ourselves on individuality but this idea lacks the inner spirituality and knowledge that we as individuals should be seeking. Since arriving in India I have peeled away a lot of my inner layers and am really working hard to achieve inner happiness. In the past I would have thought this kind of "soul searching" to be silly and

*continued...*

a waste of time, but Indians have shown me the merit in obtaining a clearer conscience and the inner peace that follows.

For me, stress and time are interlinked, where in the West the two dominate over our daily lives. I have always felt controlled by time and deadlines, never feeling that I had a moment of peace. When I arrived in Indian everything moved in such slow motion that I nearly had a heart attack from the shock. Every task seems to take forever and I struggled to see that anything was getting done. There is joke here, because Indians take so long to do things, time here is called Indian time. When you ask someone how long something will take you, they ask "Is that in Indian time?" It's a half serious question too! Indians by in large have a different concept of time, they know the value of peace. Their lunch breaks are really breaks, after a slow digestion, some people meditate and do breathing exercises, but all will take the time to enjoy the peacefulness of not working. Totally different from at home where people "scarf" down their food, or run out to do last minute tasks before running back to work. At first I thought all workers to be lazy, but soon saw the benefit of not rushing through the day. Employees are more relaxed and care free and certainly less stressed. I observed this within community settings as well, people are more relaxed and as such had calmer, clearer minds. I have tried hard in the past month to adopt this *shanty* lifestyle; I find that it has really helped me to approach situations with a clear and focused mind. I still run around too much but am at least putting conscious thought into my actions.

When I look back at this field placement, it has been one of great extremes. My emotions were tested on all fronts and my values are still

*continued...*

challenged and fought daily. This placement for me was internal rather than being about material accomplishments. I have seen some inner demons and continue to battle my preconceived ideas about the world. My practicum agency allowed me to see sides of myself that I did not know existed; beauty and the beast. As I have mentioned before, one unit lacked organization and leadership, but in many ways the land and people made up for it. In many ways this placement has been nothing but an ongoing struggle for direction and purpose and in other ways both the direction and the purpose where in front of me the whole time. I think, as students we look towards field placements as simply practical experience, an experience in which we can enhance our skills as workers. I have failed in the past to realize that these placements can also be more about life lessons and personal exploration. I am not walking away from India with a feeling of projects accomplished but a better sense of who I am as a woman, a Canadian, a spiritual person, social worker, and a human being. Having learned a lot about compassion, truth, acceptance, inner self, self doubt, anger, hatred, balance, peace and love, this field placement has brought me closer to the core being of who I am.

## Learning Goals

One of your first activities is to establish what it is that you want to learn during your international exchange. All schools of social work as well as other human service professions have developed learning goals and related activities for international exchanges that offer you a structured learning experience. The following goals come from social work but can be adapted for other human service fields.

## Nine general learning goals that you might adopt

1. Critically assess your practice experiences through peer review, constructive feedback, and consultation.
2. Learn how to participate and contribute in a seminar (in person and web-based) and create a safe learning environment for sharing with others.
3. Participate in discussions of professional issues, practice situations, and ethical dilemmas.
4. Examine and discuss the applications of theory in practice and the appropriateness of various practice methods.
5. Participate collectively and collaboratively in furthering your learning and promoting professional development.
6. Consider the CASW (Canadian Association of Social Work) code of ethics, or the code of ethics for other human service professions, and assess its application in international settings. Where applicable you will consider and apply the Code of Ethics of the host country.
7. Learn how your profession is practiced outside their societal context.
8. Critically examine the practice of your profession in the international setting—its aims, methods, values, and purposes.
9. Assess how the profession is remaining accountable to the society it serves.

## Four learning goals related to practice

1. Develop advanced comprehension of practice within an international context, which includes the articulation, application, and analysis of the knowledge base relevant to international practice.
2. Demonstrate an ability to analyze your learning needs for professional development.
3. Articulate, integrate, and defend if necessary, social work values within an international context.

4. Critique "western and northern" social work theories, values, and skills in relation to their importance or relevance to an international or national community setting.

## Three learning goals related to the international context

1. Demonstrate the ability to analyze the structure and functioning of an organization in the international community as it relates to the promotion of social well-being.
   (a) Analyze relevant policy.
   (b) Analyze the environment of the placement (organization and task domain, service networks and resources), including the political environment.
   (c) Understand the community in which the student is working, in relation to local, national, and international contexts.
2. Critique the exchange in light of different models of international development and the power issues surrounding the global context.
3. Reflect and articulate how your uniqueness (i.e., ethno-cultural, racial, sexual orientation, economic status, and life experience) has implications for the community in which you are practicing.

## Human relationships in the international context

1. Demonstrate cultural sensitivity to the host community and nation, including gaining opportunities to work with and display respect for diverse peoples.
2. Human relations or interaction skills include the ability to:
   (a) work with others to achieve the objectives of the community through strategic planning and programming;
   (b) coordinate groups, departments, factions or divisions, and to achieve community or organizational goals;

(c) evaluate the achievement of the mandate of the practice setting;

(d) purposefully interact with the environment of the practice setting;

(e) suggest changes to the organizational structure and processes, as the need arises;

(f) analyze how different value stances affect human behaviour within the practice context, including your value position;

(g) analyze interaction between the structure and processes of the practice setting and human behaviour;

(h) establish and maintain professional relationships at different levels in the setting;

(I) effectively communicate both verbally and in writing.

## How Learning Goals Can Be Achieved

The following are nine exercises that you can complete in order to achieve your learning goals. If you are required to construct a learning contract you can link these activities to your learning goals in the contract. They come from the field of social work but can be adapted for the human services.

### Integration activity 1: Presentations

While in your exchange setting you will need to know about the culture and welfare policies of your host country. As well you will be asked many questions about the culture and social welfare system of your home country. An accompanying written paper is not required, however, relevant handouts that you can take along to your host country are an essential aspect of the presentation. Feel free to use a variety of information sources both academic, homespun or from popular literature. Showing a brief, relevant video can also be an effective presentation aid.

1. The presentation will describe your evolving knowledge building related to the culture and social service system of your host culture.

2. In your presentation, offer a brief overview of your home country's social services and social welfare system.

3. Describe how you are preparing personally to meet the challenges of living and studying abroad. What personal resources will you build on, what challenges do you foresee, how will you meet these challenges? You will receive a group grade for your presentation.

## Integration activity 2: Critical incidents and summary paper

The starting point of the assignment will be narration of a critical incident in exchange. Students will reflect on their response to the critical incident in terms of their cognitive and emotional processes. Finally, students will articulate the application of social work knowledge to the incident and describe the action taken.

The format for the Critical Incident Assignment is as follows.

1. Description: Outline the background information you were working from, including a clear detailed description of the situation (omitting identifying information). Describe the setting, people involved, your own actions, actions of others and any other pertinent information.

2. Reflection: How was your understanding of "what is right" impacted by the incident? What was your role in the incident and how did you feel about your actions? Consider impact of class, ability/disability, national origin, race, language, sexual orientation, gender, age, religion, organization, and politics. Consider emotional responses such as contradictions, surprises, fear, hopes, beliefs, attitudes, and assumptions.

3. Action: What was your response? Apply professional knowledge to help you understand the situation? If faced with the same situation again, how might you respond differently?

The summary paper will note themes that emerged from the critical incidents, and your journal. It will include a critical reflection on personal assumptions and beliefs that were challenged in the field placement. A review and evaluation of your learning experience will also be included in the summary.

The following is an excerpt from a summary paper submitted by a Canadian student who completed her field placement in India, as a single mother accompanied by her two children.

I experienced many critical reflections, based on my personal assumptions and beliefs that were challenged during my field placement. It is difficult for me to pinpoint one that summarizes my entire experience. I tried to stay open-minded throughout my time in India but the challenges of meeting my and my children's needs became frustrating during various situations. It is much easier to remain open to various cultural practices when they do not directly impact you. This attitude of separation retains the notion of "us" and "them." An important piece of the international field placement is the breakdown of this separation. If you are able to stay reflective during difficult times in an international field placement you can better use your experiences to empathize and to further understand the subtleties of another culture's social work practice.

Through an international field placement one can more successfully imagine what the concerns of the people living within this particular context may be and how they experience these difficulties. During one of our site visits we were able to experience the way in which many of the sponsored children live on a daily basis. We waited

*continued...*

for two hours at the end of the day for a bus that would take us on a three-hour drive toward our home. The bus, however, never arrived and we were forced to flag down a ride. I felt very panicked and wanted to get home because my children were waiting at the crèche and I had no way to contact them. It was difficult to focus on anything else but my children. I told an agency worker I was worried about the long time I have left my children and how hungry for supper they would be and she replied, "Imagine if they were on the side of the road waiting for the bus everyday." Many of the school children were also waiting for this bus that never arrived to take them home. After getting up early in the morning to complete their chores before school the children then spent a full day at school. Many of the girls talked about their need to get home to help cook the family meal. After waiting for more than an hour many of the children slowly started their 2-3 hour walk home.

We were finally able to flag a ride down to start our way back home. Many of the children were still waiting and others had started walking home. Previous to this experience I believed that education should always be offered and that it was a priority for the quality of life for the rural children. I also had never thought about the necessity for arranged transportation for the children. I assumed that because the children went to a rural school in a small town they therefore lived within a reasonable walking distance from the school. I had also assumed school would be the main responsibility of the children. I had not realized the immense responsibilities many of the students carried in addition to their formal education. Education is an important aspect of a child's life but the

*continued...*

*Integration activity four: Useful information to know about your host and home country and city*

Prior to departure, here are 28 basic questions to ask about your host environment and culture. Many more questions will come to mind as you work through the list. Write down the answers to as many as you can. Return to the list periodically both as a guide and as a check on the progress of your quest for information.

1. How many people who are prominent in the affairs (i.e., politics, athletics, religion, and the arts) of your new environment can you name? Who is the head of state and who is the head of government?
2. What are the main political parties and what interests do they represent?
3. Who are the heroes and heroines of your new environment?
4. If going to another country than your own, can you recognize the national anthem?
5. Are other languages spoken besides the dominant language? What are the social and political implications of language usage?
6. What is the predominant religion? Have you read any of its sacred writings?
7. What are the most important religious observances and ceremonies? How regularly do people participate in them?
8. How do members of the predominant religion feel about other religions?
9. What are the most common forms of marriage ceremonies and celebrations?
10. What is the attitude toward divorce? Extra-marital relations? Plural marriage?
11. What is the attitude toward gambling?
12. What is the attitude toward drinking?
13. Is the price asked for merchandise fixed or are customers expected to bargain? How is bargaining conducted?

14. How do people organize their daily activities? What is the normal meal schedule? Is there a daytime rest period? What is the customary time for visiting friends?
15. What foods are most popular and how are they prepared?
16. What is usual dress for men and women?
17. What are the special privileges of age and sex?
18. If you are invited to dinner, should you arrive early? On time? Late?
19. On what occasions would you present gifts from people in your environment?
20. What are the important holidays? How is each observed?
21. What are the favorite leisure and recreational activities of adults? Teenagers?
22. What sports are popular?
23. How will your financial position and living conditions compare with those of the majority of people living in this country?
24. What kind of local public transportation is available and to whom?
25. What is the history of your new country and city?
26. What is the history of the relationship between your own country and your new environment?
27. What is the present relationship between your own country and your new environment?
28. What are the important universities of the country and where are they located?

*Integration activity five: Helpful questions for you to ask your academic or agency sherpas or other students who have participated in an international exchange*

The following 18 questions, intended for consideration while you are living in your host country, are more comprehensive than the prior list and help you to think about the kinds of information you will want to know concerning your host community and country. We suggest you maintain a journal to record your responses to these questions as they may guide your behavior and provide insights into, what at times, may be confusing responses of members of your host community.

1. *General attitudes and values*
   - What are the attitudes and values towards privacy, politeness, friendship, demonstration of wealth, punctuality, work, obligation, race, minorities, crime, violence, military and police?

2. *Greetings, farewell, and leave-taking*
   - How do introductions, greetings and leave-taking vary among new people, acquaintances and close friends?
   - What are some gender, age or race differences in terms of greetings, farewells and leave-taking?
   - When are titles used? (ie. Mr. Mrs. Dr.)
   - What are the conventions in terms of standing, sitting, distance and touching?

3. *Visiting*
   - When visiting, what is acceptable or inappropriate in regard to topics of conversation, gift-giving, compliments on possessions, family circumstances, local and national circumstances?
   - What table manners are acceptable?
   - Are there unique behavioral expectations at parties and social events?
   - Are thank-you notes expected?

4. *Public addresses*
   - If you are required to give a public address, what subjects and illustrations should be avoided?
   - What mannerisms and gestures are inappropriate?
   - How will you work with interpreters?

5. *Business meetings*
   - What are the conventions in terms of time, place, setting and format?
   - What are usual ways of beginning and ending meetings?
   - What is acceptable in terms of eye contact, posture and seating arrangements?
   - Are refreshments expected?

6. *Gestures*
   What is the convention related to posture, motion of arms, hands, fingers, legs and feet?
   When is it acceptable to touch, embrace or point?
   - How are things handled as for example in passing and receiving?

7. *Personal appearance*
   - What is expected in terms of formal and informal clothing?
   - What is the place of jewelry and other adornments (i.e., tattoos)?
   - What are the gender differences in terms of appropriate attire?

8. *Language and religion*
   - What common languages are written and spoken?
   - What are some common phrases?
   - Is the question of language a source of conflict?
   - What religions are practiced? Is religion a source of conflict?
   - What are some common rituals and taboos?
   - What is the relationship between predominant groups and minorities? What is the impact of this relationship?
   - What are the special holy days and the accompanying observances?
   - What are the 'luck' myths?

9. *Families*
   - What is the status of children in your host country?
   - What gender differences are evident in parenting?
   - What are the expectations of children in terms of authority figures?
   - How would you describe the parenting style of parents in the host country? What is the impact of this parenting style?
   - Are there rites and rituals of entrance at various development levels?
   - What is the status of the elderly?
   - What are the inheritance customs?

10. *Dating, courtship and marriage*
    - What are the influences of parents and peers before and after marriage?
    - What are common dating and courtship activities?
    - What are acceptable and unacceptable displays of affection?
    - What are some prerequisites to marriage (eg. dowries, rites, rituals)?
    - What is the attitude to abortion?
    - What is the attitude towards divorce?
    - What are the attitudes towards gays, lesbians and the transgendered?

11. *Diet and dwellings*
    - What are the challenges and opportunities related to diet and dwellings?
    - What is the average diet, meal size and scheduling?
    - What special foods are reserved for guest and ritual occasions?

12. *Work*
    - How do work expectations vary in terms of age, sex, status and class?
    - What are the main occupations and industries?

- What is a typical work schedule?
- How do environment, climate and government impact work conditions?
- What are some issues related to work compensation in relation to gender, age, race, ability and sexual orientation?

13. *Recreation and leisure*
   - What are some common family and social recreational activities?
   - Are there exclusions in terms of participation? What is the impact of this exclusion?
   - Who are some well-known artists and athletes?

14. *History and government*
   - What is the attitude towards the government?
   - What is the attitude towards other nations?
   - What is the impact of major historical events?
   - What are the systems of national, regional and local governments?
   - Is there an emphasis on civil liberties?

15. *Education*
   - What is the attitude towards education?
   - What are the barriers to education? What is the impact of these barriers?
   - Are educational resources seen as adequate?
   - What is the status of public and private education?

16. *Transportation and communication*
   - What is the cost and scope of individual and group travel?
   - What is the quality of the road systems?
   - What is the impact of class, race, gender and dis/ability on transportation?
   - How available is access to the internet? What is the impact of this availability?
   - Is the postal system effective?

17. *Health and sanitation*
    - What is the nature of access to health care? How does this access impact citizens of the host country?
    - What is the attitude towards sanitation? What is the impact of this attitude?
    - What are the implications for visitors?

18. *Geography and climate*
    - What is the historical and contemporary impact of geography?
    - What is the impact of climate on economics and lifestyle?
    - What should visitors be aware of or particularly avoid?

## Integrative activity six: Self reflection on cultural awareness

Consider the following description of cultural awareness. Write a two page reflective essay applying these concepts to your experience.

## Four levels of cultural awareness

As you go through the cycle of adjustment, your awareness of the host culture naturally increases. This awareness tend to progress through a series of levels, which are described below. Each level corresponds to a phase or phases in the cycle of adjustment.

1. *Unconscious incompetence*

   Unconscious incompetence is also known as a state of blissful ignorance. At this stage, you are unaware of cultural differences. It does not occur to you that you may be making cultural mistakes or that you may be misinterpreting much of the behaviour going on around you. You have no reason not to trust your instincts.

2. *Conscious incompetence*

   You now realize that differences exist between the way you and the local people behave, although you understand very little about what these differences are, how numerous they might be, or how deep they might go. You know there is a problem, but you are not sure about the size of it. You are not so sure of your instincts anymore, and you realize that some things you do not understand. You may start to worry about how hard it is going to be to understand these people.

3. *Conscious competence*

You know cultural difference exists, you know what some of these differences are, and you try to adjust your own behaviour accordingly. Conscious competence does not come naturally yet – you have to make an effort to behave in culturally appropriate ways – but you are much more aware of how your behaviour is perceived by the local people. You are in the process of replacing old instincts with new ones. You know now that you will be able to understand the local people if you can remain objective.

4. *Unconscious competence*

You no longer have to think about what you are doing in order to do the right thing. Culturally appropriate behaviour is now second nature to you; you can trust your instincts because they have been reconditioned by the new culture. It takes little effort for you to be culturally sensitive.

## Integrative activity seven: Self reflection

Self reflection is an important aspect of all social work practice and is a powerful way to develop culturally sensitivity and effectiveness in international social work practice. Friere (1973) argued that it can help individuals better understand their bias and social conditioning in a potentially transformative way and develop a critical consciousness about issues such as class, status, gender, sexual orientation, race, and ethnicity.

Other scholars (Schon, 1983) believed that self-reflection can enhance creativity, critical thinking, and the ability to empathize.

As a student you may become disoriented in your new culture and are a risk for behaving in ways that your academic or agency Sherpas may deem as inappropriate and counterproductive in your exchange setting. Self-reflection can mitigate this risk.

Writing can facilitate self-reflection and self-discovery and reveal the complexity of your exchange experience. Here are some ways to harness the power of writing.

- Poetry can help you explore, for example, your strengths, potential, mistakes, bias, and values.
- Write about your first day or your first week. Start with prompts such as "I felt..."; "I noticed..."; "I smelled..."; "I tasted..."; "I liked..."; and "I'm worried about...."
- Write a poem to or about your client, your field instructor, a colleague, or someone you noticed on the street. This poem will most likely remain in your possession. You are not required to give it to the person.

### Integrative activity eight: Write an essay

The International Federation of Social Work (IFSW ) states that unjust policies and practices that support negative discrimination must be challenged while those that recognize and enhance cultural diversity, an inclusive society, and equitable distribution of resources must be promoted (see http://www.ifsw.org).

Select a topic that is of particular interest to you such as poverty, women's issues, children's rights, ability and disability, gender roles, sexual orientation, the elderly, or displaced persons.

Compare the social policies and practices of your home and host country in terms of fairness and equitable distribution of resources in areas such as health care, public safety, peace, the legal system, pollution, education, and politics. Consider your analysis in light of the country's history of war, natural resources, gender roles, race, religion, and global relationships.

The following questions can guide your thinking.

- What is the historic involvement of the home country with the host country? Speculate on how this relationship influenced the reception you received in the host country?
- Is there differential access to food, health care, housing, and education?
- What are the subtle practices of privilege? Is privilege based on discriminatory practices?
- How does oppression based on poverty, race, and ethnic identity limit the choices of the group under study?

## Integrative activity nine: Into the community

- Interview a host country national about their perspectives on social problems. What are the strengths of their country? What challenges do the face? What are their wishes for change? Write down the essence of the interview, record your thoughts and feelings and consider the interview in light of issues such as oppression, gender roles, equity, privilege, and power. Pedagogy of the Oppressed by Paulo Freire (1998) is an excellent accompaniment to this integrative activity.
- Visit and learn about the positive aspects of community life by participating in community celebrations, visiting historic sites, art galleries, museums, and attending religious services.
- Interview a social worker from three different agencies in your host country to learn about their roles, work challenges, rewards of their work and the cultural perspectives about giving and receiving help.
- At the end of your placement, describe the nature of your relationships with nationals, col-

leagues at your field agency and clients. What did you appreciate about these relationships? What would you do differently?

- Create a community map of social services.

## Other integrative activities

Other integrative activities include case studies, journals, portfolio, and e-chats. Posting excerpts from the case studies and journal entries on an online discussion forum can be a powerful collaborative learning opportunity.

## The Question of Language

The question of language is a source of uncertainly among academic Sherpas. Must a student, they ask, be fluent in the language of the host country? What language skill level is considered adequate? For example, while Canadian students studying in a non-English speaking host country may have developed language skills that support ordering meals, shopping and travelling, is it realistic to expect that they should engage with proficiency in therapeutic encounters that require the expression of abstract ideas? Often times even English speakers notice and are surprised by language usages as they move from one country to another.

> *One student wrote:*
>
> I woke up to realize there was no hot water in the building. I had to wash my hair in cold water. I realized later it was scheduled; I just never paid attention to the signs everywhere because I couldn't read them!

In a study conducted by the authors of this book, we found that the lack of language proficiency was a major stumbling block for some students completing an international exchange. We found that students felt frustrated when they weren't able to engage in tradi-tionally defined therapeutic interactions and provide in-depth emotional help because of language limitations (Schwartz et al., 2011). Other authors found similar results. In his description of an exchange organized within Europe, Horncastle (1994: 313) stated that his students felt "frustrated and a feeling of being deskilled" due to a lack of competency in other European lan-guages. On the other hand, Gilin and Young (2009) felt that their students involved in an exchange developed more empathy for the non-English speaking clients they would work with in the future than they would have had if they had not experienced the frustration of struggling to be understood in a foreign language and the experi-ence of being "the other" in a different culture.

> *One of our students wrote:*
>
> Lately I have been thinking about what it must be like for immigrants arriving in Canada. I thought I could see before but now I really see how scary it must be for them. My friend E, who is doing just what I am but in Belgium described it perfectly: it is like having no ears and no mouth – all I have are my eyes. I cannot understand others and they cannot understand me. It is sheer frus-tration when you are trying to get help, find some-thing, ask anything when you cannot be understood or vice versa. It is really hard to hear people going by in large groups, laughing and speaking in Polish and I think to myself, how am I ever going to fit in to that? Well if anything this trip will really help me to empathize with people from other countries coming to Canada.

It is extremely important to communicate in the language of the host country. It is considered a signifi-cant means of exercising power (Pugh, 2003). Wilfing (2003) describes how power is equalized between a social worker and the people they are working with when that person is allowed to showcase their capabilities as native speakers to the social worker developing their language skills. Pugh (2003) notes in another article that faster rates of speech are ranked more favourably and slower rates of speech are associated with uncertainty and lack of knowledge. This will affect the perceived competence of social workers struggling to communicate with an unfamiliar language.

There are many ways that your academic Sherpa can help you to brush up your language skills. A Canadian exchange student completing a field placement in Brussels became acutely aware of the subtle differences in language and responded by creating the following chart.

| Belge term | English translation | Canadian Social Work term | Comments |
|---|---|---|---|
| • étranger | • foreigner<br>• alien | • in the country temporarily – "visitor"<br>• newly in the country permanently – "newcomer"<br>• in the country as a citizen of Canada with origins in another country – "Canadian" or "-Canadian" if the client prefers to be recognized as such, i.e., African-Canadian | • All of the English versions of the French documentation use the term Alien, which in English means a being from another planet. The Canadian terms or phrases that describe individuals originating from countries other than Canada who use excessive wordage. The result is less of a label and more of an exclusive description. |

*continued...*

| | | | |
|---|---|---|---|
| • prostitue<br>• prostitu-<br>tion | • prostitute<br>• prostitu-<br>tion | • sex worker<br>• sex work | • The Canadian term is broad and general. It is meant to include those who provide sex or sex-related services in exchange for money, shelter, food, or drugs as a victim of the sex trade or by choice as a profession. |
| • toxico-<br>mane<br>• toxicoma-<br>nia | • drug addict<br>• drug addic-<br>tion | • person who uses drugs<br>• addiction issues | |
| • 1les sans-<br>papiers<br>• les illégaux | • those with-<br>out papers<br>• the illégales | • person/client unable to secure citizenship | • Typically Canadian social work descriptions are constructed not to categorize the person or group but rather the situation they are in. For this reason, a phrase is usually preferred over a term. |
| • réfugies | • refugees | • displaced persons | |

## A student narrative on language

I realized very early on that I will have to let go off any expectations or ideas I had about what this whole experience should look like, especially my field placement, in order to truly embrace this experience and learn from it. It has given me this amazing freedom and I am becoming more and more open to new challenges, and instead of fearing them and try to run away from them, I try to face them and tackle them, all the while not trying to be so hard on myself. This is very new for me and sort of revolutionary in a way, as I have always been a perfectionist in many ways and have always wanted to avoid getting involved in situations where I have little experience. I know this post is supposed to be about a "story," but really, there are so many, I am not sure which one to pick! Maybe I will share with you what I have been doing in the last week. I have just returned from a week-long camp with 44 kids and youth and five staff! This is a crazy ratio considering that all these kids come from very diverse backgrounds and almost all have huge behavioural, social, and emotional problems. Anyway, I was quite terrified of the thought at first of spending a week in an all-polish speaking environment when I am still not so confident with my polish. It ended up being a fantastic experience though! Pretty much everything I did that week was out of my comfort zone but it was so amazing, I learned how to just relax and enjoy being uncomfortable. I had to throw any ideas of what my role as a social worker should be at this camp out of the window, because it was impossible for me to do there what I would do in Canada. In Canada, I would have probably been a lot more focused on

*continued...*

the program, trying to apply different behavioural modification techniques and being a positive role model. All this, I had to do in a more improvised manner and with many limitations (again, as a result of the language barrier).

It was a wonderful time sharing, laughing, and of learning together. There were times when the kids became my little teachers; teaching me how to speak Polish (I in turn taught them some English) or one day, we went to a skating ring and I don't know how to skate but I said to myself, "why not, I will try this, since I have embarked on this journey of embracing new things" so they taught me how to skate! I think this gave them some sense of accomplishment and pride as they shared their knowledge and skills with me. All I had to do was be myself with them and be real with them and show them that I care, and they responded to that and we were able to connect even without using too many words.

Some of the kids and youth had big problems with swearing and using profanities, and I did not know the meaning of all the swear words and slang in Polish just yet. So there were funny moments when I had no idea what they were saying. Once, a little kid looked at me and said, "Pani Rana, they are swearing. They shouldn't be. You should tell them to stop." I would have a good laugh about it afterwards because part of my work was to correct inappropriate behaviour such as swearing. How could I do that if I didn't know the swear words?

## Seven language tips for students

1. Plan ahead. Take a language course prior to departure.
2. Enroll in a language class while in your host country.
3. When all else fails, write it instead of verbalizing it.
4. Repeat information to check that you have heard it correctly.
5. Speak slowly and wait for an answer.
6. Recruit assistance from other students who are happy to provide extra language support.
7. Remember that language challenges in your host country can undermine your self-confidence and contribute to culture shock because the spoken language is fast paced, there are many discipline specific words with which you have not familiarity, and you will become exhausted from using the host country language all day.

Six language tips for academic and agency sherpas

1. Use short sentences.
2. Use an active rather than a passive voice when giving instructions.
3. Avoid use of metaphors that require considerable cultural knowledge such as in English "*back to square one*" or "*searching for a needle in the haystack.*"
4. Create a discipline-specific wordlist and develop a signal system such that the student can alert you when she does not understand.
5. Understand your assumptions about learning, writing and communication styles, and beliefs about how one is to behave in the workplace.
6. Notice possible cultural differences in relation to communication and behaviour such as the use of silences; pauses; taking turns; showing respect to peers and authority figures; and sharing opinions.

## Conclusion

This chapter has a number of learning activities. Some of them will help you develop a learning contract. This is a document that you will negotiate with the person supervising you in your exchange. Others are activities that you can include in your learning contract. We cannot emphasize enough the importance of learning the language of your host country so that you can truly make a contribution in your exchange setting and so that you can get the most out of your exchange.

# Reflection Questions

1. Have I developed clear learning goals that are suitable for an international exchange?
2. Have I reviewed the learning goals with my academic Sherpa?
3. What challenges do I foresee in maintaining a working relationship with my academic Sherpa and in completing my assignments? What is my strategy for meeting these challenges?
4. Do I have a beginning understanding of my host country's culture?
5. Based on what I know about myself, what will be some of my day to day living challenges in my host country?
6. If I do not have a beginning literacy in the language of my host culture, how will I communicate with its citizens? How important is a beginning knowledge of the host country language to success in my field placement?

# Chapter 5

## Preparing for an International Exchange: Opportunities and Challenges

Preparing for an international exchange is time consuming and should start as soon as possible. Not only does it require early planning, it also requires making sure that family and friends are aware of the exchange and that appropriate arrangements are made, for instance, with your job, relationships, and other issues in life that need to be addressed and finalized. The following is a list of arrangements that you should address before leaving the country; arrangements when in your host country; and resettling into your own country afterwards.

## Arrangements Prior to Departure

### Risk management

When you are overseas, there are a number of issues to consider concerning risk. Living in a relatively safe city in Canada, many of these issues are taken for granted. You should be prepared to take extra precautions while you are abroad to ensure your safety. When we consider danger in foreign countries, we often think of high profile acts of violence such as terrorist attacks. While this may be a possibility in some countries, you are more likely to be the victim of more common crimes like robbery, mugging, and sexual assault. In addition, you may be inclined to take more risks than you would at home. You are strongly advised to go to the Risk Management Office at your University, which should have some information on travel risks associated with various countries, before leaving Canada. The Government of

Canada website also has a section called Advisories which list risks associated with various countries. Be sure to know how to access emergency assistance through the Canadian consulate in the country where you are living.

## Travel Documents

- Passport
- Visa
- Extra Passport Photos
- International Student Identity Card
- Youth Hostel Card

- Home Drivers Liscense
- International Drivers Liscense
- Medical Card
- Eye Prescription
- Other Prescription

### Passport

Apply for your passport at the Passport Office in your city or at a travel agent that provides this service. It can take a month or longer to process depending on the time of year. You will need your passport to obtain a Student Visa for most countries.

### Visa

Please check with the country consulate concerning the type of visa you will need in order to engage in a field placement in that particular country. Be sure to find out, as early as possible, what is needed so that you are not waiting at the last minute for the appropriate visa. The agency in which you are doing your exchange may be able to obtain the visa for you. Lonely Planet website also gives visa information. Consider the following three things to remember regarding visas.

1. Depending on the country to which you are traveling, you will need to obtain the appropriate visa before you arrive.
2. You must determine the policy of the country to which you are traveling well before you leave

since some countries require that you apply for your visa 6-8 weeks or more before you leave.

3. Contact the embassy or consulate of the country to which you are traveling in order to obtain your visa.

If you plan to travel after your field placement you may need to apply to several countries for entry visas. This is usually done at the embassy in the country where you are based. You should take a few passport photos in case they are needed for visa applications. Do not assume that you can enter any country just on the basis of your passport. Check out the requirements before you go.

Be aware that you may need to have proof of finances and health insurance before you are allowed to apply for a student visa. Proof of finances will normally include your letter of acceptance from your agency, photocopies of your bank statements, and other documents.

### International student identification

Pick up an International Student Identification Card (ISIC) from a local travel agency like Travel Cuts (in Canada), which may have a branch on your university campus. It may entitle you to some discounts when traveling and is widely recognized as proof of studentship.

### Youth hostel care

You should consider buying a Youth Hostel Card if you are planning to travel before, during or after your field placement. This will allow you to board inexpensively in any countries that provide youth hostels. You may also need to take advantage of temporary housing options if your other accommodations are not ready when you arrive.

### Driver's license

In general, your Canadian driver's license should be sufficient for any driving you wish to do abroad. However, you might wish to obtain an International Drivers License just in case. You can obtain this through your automobile association. Driving can be costly and often public transportation is more efficient and safer.

While you are getting these documents ready, there are two important things to keep in mind:

1.  You must notify your agency of your arrival dates and times. If they offer airport pickup and temporary accommodation they will need the details of your travel well in advance. In some countries taxis are not reliable or safe. If at all possible, arrange for someone you know who is safe and reliable to pick you up at the airport. If not, take a licensed taxi.

2.  You should make a photocopy of your airline ticket as well as the issuing agent. Put one copy in your suitcase and keep one with you. If lost, these things could make it easier to replace. In addition, be sure to have adequate travel insurance to cover your baggage, theft, and airline ticket cancellation.

## Health and medical concerns

Preparing a health package can help you to adjust to a new environment. Clean water (water filter), healthy food (know what is safe), a first aid kit, books to read, and pictures from home all help in a student's physical and emotional adjustment while in a new environment.

You will need to get the appropriate injections for the country in which you are traveling. The nurses at your local travel clinic or university health service will need to know exactly which inoculations you require. Book your appointment as early as possible because it can take a couple of weeks, particularly during the high tourist season.

Before traveling get information about health issues in that country and community. The World Health Organization travel and health advisory can guide you in learning about current health issues worldwide. Most travel agencies provide health insurance at a cost. The Lonely Planet and other travel guides also give suggestions on pre-departure health information. These guides also list the names of body parts in the language of the country, as well as questions to ask medical personnel regarding what conditions you may experience.

*One students wrote:*

> While I understand how difficult it is to communicate your needs in a foreign language, I feel that if I was in an emergency, I would have enough skills to be able to communicate about my health challenges, even if I could not describe them with the advanced vocabulary that I would use in English. However, I would feel ill at ease if the medical staff could not explain to me what they were doing if they were treating me. I would feel very vulnerable and lack a sense of control. I am incredibly fortunate to fluently speak English which, while it is a minority language in the world, is also the universal one that many people try to learn. If I was in a situation where I needed medical attention, I would probably ask for an interpreter, but I sincerely doubt that I would insist that it is my human right for me to get medical treatment in my native language if it is not widely spoken in that particular country.

## Medical and dental checkup

It is a good idea to have a medical and dental checkup before you go. If you have a medical condition, ask your doctor to write a letter outlining the situation and what treatments or prescriptions you require. Other points to ponder:

- Take a copy of eye prescriptions with you in case you need to replace your eyeglasses while away.

- Be aware that if you have a pre-existing condition such as diabetes, depression, or an eating disorder, going abroad may cause increased stress and ultimately aggravate your condition. You should discuss your concerns with your physician and get some advice on how to cope with stress while abroad.
- If you have a disability (physical or learning) you may have to make arrangements for special assistance and accommodation.

## Phones and internet

Many countries use cell phones for communication, either talking or texting. If you wish to use your own phone in another country, then your phone needs to have a SIM card and be unlocked. Once you are in the country, buy a SIM card at a local phone distributor so you will only be charged local prices. If not, you will be charged huge amounts of money. You may be able to buy a phone cheaply in the host country. This may be more cost effective than getting your phone unlocked or buying an unlocked phone in Canada. iPads are also good to take as they will connect you to home where there is WiFi. A phone or iPad are useful because internet cafes might not be available.

## Financial matters

### Banking

You must decide how you will conduct your banking while abroad. This includes currency exchanges, banking machines, credit cards, and paying bills. Ask your bank how to transfer funds. It is also helpful to email a bank in the host country in order to ensure that you bring funds in a form that they will accept.

### Taxes

You will have to file an income tax return while out of the country. We recommend that you keep any receipts for major purchases to show Canada Customs upon return. Make sure these are marked "Used Personal Purchases."

## Home and family issues

Discuss your travel plans with your family, faculty Sherpa, significant others, partner, and friends. Make sure you have their support, as it will make the transition easier. Provide these people with copies of important documents such as your passport, visa, credit cards, travelers cheques, emergency contacts, and travel itinerary. Fill in all of your university information and risk forms.

## Will and power of attorney

Although we hope to never lose a student on an international exchange, it is a good idea to prepare a will before you leave. You may also want to assign "power of attorney" to a family member you trust. This will give them the authority to deal with any issues that may arise while you are away such as signing legal documents, paying bills, accessing accounts, and picking up cheques.

## Packing and baggage

The most common problem when packing is taking too much with you. If you cannot carry your luggage around the block at home, you will not be able to handle it by yourself when trying to get on the plane, or from the plane to a train or bus. If you plan to travel during or after your field placement period, you may wish to use a backpack.

*Consider the following ten packing and baggage tips*:

1. Find the baggage restrictions policy of the airline.
2. Be sure to note what extra charges there are for oversized baggage.
3. It might make sense to mail some articles to yourself that will arrive after you do or to purchase these items after you arrive.
4. If you are thinking of mailing some items to yourself, be sure to find out the customs regulations of the country to which you are traveling.

5. Put a copy of your travel plans in your check-in baggage.
6. Take some time to study the culture and determine what is appropriate to wear. Ask your agency Sherpa what is appropriate to wear for work.
7. It is a good idea to know a little about the climate.
8. Consider a money belt or pouch to carry your documents when in transit. It is unwise to carry large amounts of cash with you.
9. It would be advisable to prepare a personal envelope with the following items included: Photocopy of passport, name of person to contact in case of an emergency, preferably in Canada and in the country/community where you will be working, blood type, written information on any special health problems, copy of proof of Health Care and extended health care (e.g., Blue Cross Coverage), and a contact number where you can be reached by your university. This could be held in the general office of your program.
10. Bring gifts from your own country to give to the people who are involved with your international exchange. These can be simple things from a dollar store that have the Canadian flag on them or more elaborate gifts.

## Arriving In Host Country

There will be many adjustments to make in the first 2-3 months upon arriving at your host country. With the support from your host university, exchange agency, and from family and friends at home, these initial adjustments will be less traumatic. Everyone will experience challenges with adjusting to varying degrees. It helps to know that problems will arise and to know what it is you are experiencing. This difficulty in confronting and coping with new cultural circumstances has been termed "culture shock" or more recently "cultural adaptation." It affects nearly every traveler; even experienced ones. Millions of people overcome this challenge, and you will too. The U-curve was first introduced by Lysgaard (1955) and supported by Oberg (1960) in helping to identify stages of cultural adaptation. The stages were (1) honeymoon; (2) culture shock; (3) adjustment; and (4) mastery. An intercultural experience is a potent and personal teacher; it forces you into realizations about others and about yourself. "Culture shock is not simply meeting the new and unknown but is also a consequence of the loss of the old and familiar" (Kealey, 2001, p 45). Indeed, the greatest "shock" may not be encountering a different culture but in recognizing how your own culture shapes you and what you do. This difficulty might also be termed "role shock." Many times what is really "shocking" or surprising to people is not necessarily the new culture, rather it is a change of roles they are forced to assume within their family or organizational structure as it functions in the new culture.

In recent years, there has been criticism around the use of simplistic models of adaptation to explain complex experiences around cross-cultural experiences (Gaw, 2000; Kealey, 2001; La Brack, 2012; Szkudlarek, 2010). Martin and Harrell (2004) identify three functional categories for adaptation: (1) affective (psychological wellbeing of the individual); (2) behavioural (acquiring new and forgetting old behaviours); and (3) cognitive (expectations and cultural identity). All three categories affect the outcomes of adaptation. Critics argue that the U-curve is a simplistic model of cultural transitions and we should keep in mind that adaptation is much more complex than these models imply. Kealey (2001) studied Canadian technical advisors overseas in regards to attributes that are important for cross-cultural effectiveness. He tested the stages of cross-cultural adaptation to see if the traditional U-curve perspective is accurate. What he found challenged the approach. Only 10 percent of the sample (277 advisors) reported patterns of satisfaction that corresponded to the U-curve. He found that these Canadian advisors "experienced high levels of stress, sharp contrast to the initial 'high' suggested early on by the U-curve" (p. 60-61). Although this study is over 20-years-old, the results are valuable when processing your experience overseas.

In summary, these stages are not experienced to the same degree and some individuals may not experience them at all.

Some helpful questions concerning cultural adaptation are as follows: 1) Is it possible to fit in everywhere – to be an "international" person? (2) Are there people who can ignore their own culture and adapt completely to other ways of life? It is doubtful. Each of us has attitudes, emotions, prejudices, habits, and mannerisms that are as much a product of our culture as is the language we speak or the beliefs we accept and react to regularly.

Knowing and using parts of a language does not insure that native speakers will understand. When we consider that communication includes all behaviour and circumstances, it is clear that knowledge of the written and spoken language may by itself be insufficient. Communication depends on hundreds of signs and symbols that are largely recognized subconsciously. The signs or cues that you use to orient yourself include: when and

*One Finish student in Canada describes her experience:*

I was so clueless about everything and had to learn to do things in a totally different way than in my own country. I was a good student and worker in Finland and now in Canada I struggle. Of course, with time I got better, but never as good as I could be because of all the language and cultural barriers. Anyway, it was a good to face challenges because it forced me to learn.

how to greet people, eat food, get from place to place, and talk informally with others. When you enter another culture, many of the cues that you are familiar with may not exist or have different meanings. The mental and emotional adjustment required of those living abroad is real.

The first step toward adjustment is accepting that it is a challenge. It is a temporary condition that will pass as you become familiar with the language, mannerisms, and local customs. You may not like to believe that you are experiencing emotional stress, but it is wise to admit it when it happens. Even mild adjustments generally involve the four phases outlined below, and occur during the earliest part of a new encounter. The different phases are only general guidelines, you may or may not experience all of these phases, and they are not necessarily experienced sequentially. Some people may experience these phases more than once, at different times during their exchange, or not at all.

## PHASE I: "How quaint!"

The spirit of adventure carries you through the "honeymoon" phase. Generally someone will help you get settled, you will be excited about the "newness of it all," and possibly things will go well. You are comfortable as long as you can see similarities between your native culture and your new environment. Normally this phase does not last if you remain abroad and cope with this novel reality.

## PHASE II: "It's just not like home"

When the newness and excitement wear off (from a few hours to six months), the real challenge starts. As you begin to see and feel differences, you may feel disoriented. Language offers the greatest security in personal relationships. If you do not have an adequate interpreter, you will be stripped of your primary means of interaction. It is frustrating to be unable to display your education and intelligence; symbols that give you status and security back home. Culture shock is a psychological reaction that is manifested in physical behaviours. Another sign that you are in the critical second phase of cultural adjustment is the tendency to chat with other "foreigners" and complain about the country and the people.

You may be excessively concerned with washing hands, the cleanliness of drinking water, food, dishes, and bedding; as a result, you may fear physical contact with attendants. You can be identified by your absent-minded, far-away stare, and you may feel a dependence upon long-term residents from your country. You may experience fits of anger over delays and other minor frustrations, or fear the possibility of being cheated, robbed or injured. You will show great concern over minor pains. Finally, your frustration will be highlighted by a terrible longing to be back home, eat familiar food, visit familiar places and relatives, and talk to people with ease.

This phase may also be characterized as "culture fatigue"; similar to battle fatigue. You just get tired of not being home. In spite of your ability to cope on a daily basis or in specific cases, you eventually become generally uncomfortable.

*One EU student who came to Canada wrote:*

I was definitely not prepared when I came to Canada. I thought I was prepared but the reality was a total surprise to me. In the beginning I was excited and open-minded (a "honeymoon" experience, I later learned).

I found the social work classes to be interesting and practical and was amazed at how developed social work was in Canada.

There was so much to learn and I wanted to experience everything. But my body didn't seem to be working effectively. I had times when I felt suddenly tired and would fall asleep in the day, which was not typical for me. I didn't know

*continued...*

about jet lag. I had never flown in a plane and did not know to take time to rest. I felt trapped in my own body. It took me a week to adjust.

When I adjusted to the time difference, I started to experience emotional and cultural stress. My body reacted so that I had no appetite, I couldn't fall asleep, and I had nightmares. I also had headaches, couldn't concentrate, and felt exhausted.

I felt sad and tired but tried to pretend that everything was not so bad. That's our culture – you don't ask anyone for help and you pretend to be self-reliant. I didn't want others to know how I was feeling. I didn't know how to explain how I felt and was worried about how others would react.

I felt homesick and lonely. I was critical of Canadian culture and values, where everyone is independent and self-sufficient. I idealized my home culture and traditions. I begin to spend more and more time with the people from my culture.

I got a lot of support from everyday people I met in the town where I lived. I coped by staying in contact with my family by internet, but still felt overwhelmed. Then, I started applying what I was learning in my social work classes – I took care of my body, ate healthy food, and got exercise. I was so thankful to my Canadian host family who gave me healthy food.

Although my body got better, I still felt like I was at the bottom of a very big hole with all my heavy baggage. I felt stupid because I couldn't think quickly. Finally, I asked for help at the university's Wellness Center. With their help, I decided to work on myself and benefit as much as possible from my stay in Canada.

*continued...*

I still had my ups and downs but I got better. Then I became afraid to return to Poland. I looked forward to seeing my friends and family but knew I had changed a lot and would have to readjust again – physically, emotionally, and spiritually. I find the spiritual part to be the most challenging because I know how difficult it was for me to merge Canadian values, and I'm not sure how long it will take and how painful it will be to try to live with them in my home country.

## PHASE III: "It's starting to make sense"

The first sign of your recovery from Phase II is the return of your sense of humour. You enter the third phase when you begin to recognize communicative cues: people's faces, actions, and tones. And you begin to piece together a pattern of behaving and living. As you master the language, you begin to communicate more effectively. When you build your familiarity and knowledge, you find yourself making it through each day with greater ease. Many government and private organizations specialize in preparing Canadians to adjust to their experience abroad. One such program suggests to its participants that to be adequate "culture shock absorbers," they have to first develop self-awareness – an understanding of their own feelings and cultural patterns, what offends or confuses them, and why they feel dissatisfied, as discussed on the preceding pages. It is suggested that visitors temporarily suspend judgment about conditions they find unpleasant or confusing until they learn more about the people and the reasons they think and act as they do. The recovery stage progresses rapidly as visitors begin to empathize with the people of the host culture. Students imaginatively meet each challenge or perplexing situation, concerned more with gaining new insights and new friends than with feeling sorry about their own inadequacies or the country's "oddities." They remember who "the foreigner" really is.

## PHASE IV: "I understand"

The fourth and final phase will carry you through your stay abroad. Now that you are willingly adjusting to the new culture, you can accept it as "just another way" of living. It does not mean that you are enthusiastic about everything the people do or about the way they do it; it does mean that you can accept and understand the differences. You will still have moments of strain and times of misunderstanding, but you will begin to feel more "comfortable" and will genuinely enjoy yourself. Some "take to" another culture sooner than others do. Then again, you may adapt more quickly to one culture than to another. The more a culture differs from your own, the more difficult you might expect your adjustment to be. However, if you have had previous intercultural experience, you will probably have fewer problems than a "first timer."

## Cultivating Awareness

Furthermore, you will adapt readily to varying cultures to the extent that you have the following three general characteristics:

1. Awareness of self. You need a positive self-image and must have the ability to adapt. You need to be emotionally stable in situations that challenge personal feelings. Self-motivation allows you to act positively rather than react negatively to a strange environment.
2. Awareness of others. A tolerance of ambiguity and uncertainty makes it easier to understand others.
3. Awareness of circumstances. Sensitivity to circumstances allows you to pick up behaviour patterns more quickly. If you look, listen, and appropriately imitate, you will communicate more effectively with people around you, and you will be able to establish pleasant relationships.

Adjusting to a new culture can be a powerful learning tool. While you may suffer from temporary frustration, discomfort, and anxiety, these feelings can facilitate self-understanding and personality development. Because you must deal with the situations yourself, you will learn. The very experiences that disrupt your personality and its relationship to your surroundings will be the basis upon which you can build an expanded, enlightened personality. Half the battle of cultural adjustment is won if you realize that you will experience it. And the other half is won by using your cultural sensitivity to learn and make the adjustment a positive experience.

### Nine Ways to adapting to a new environment

1. Develop a spirit of adventure.
2. Keep an open mind.
3. Get out and get involved.
4. Show curiosity by looking, feeling, tasting, and asking.
5. Make friends with a number of different groups.
6. "Learn" the language.
7. Make an assumption and use it as a guide:
   - What they do is different or similar from what Canadians do.
   - Observe the differences and similarities.
   - Try to understand the differences and similarities.
   - When in doubt, ask for clarification.
   - Whom do you ask?
8. Enhance certain attributes and make effective use of them, for example:
   T = Tolerance
   I = Insightfulness
   T = Tactfulness
   A = Acceptance of Ambiguity
   C = Cross-cultural communication
   H = Humor
9. Be yourself

# Cultural Adaptation Coping Methods

We will elaborate on the nine tips to adapting to a new environment in the following section by focusing on cultural adaptation.

*Participation with locals:* Instead of sitting around reflecting on your sorry state, go out and socialize with locals. Learn about your new country and local community.

*Patience:* Sometimes this means going with the flow and not analyzing so much; you will figure it out as you go along!

*Language learning:* Language and culture are inexplicably tied together. Learning even a few words before you go is an excellent way to connect with people.

*Go with low expectations:* Expect difficulties. Tone down your expectations of what might occur. Every country and culture has its problems and day-to-day realities.

*Be an active observer of detail:* Being an "active observer" can be a great way to learn as opposed to shutting yourself off from experiences with the host culture.

*Befriend a sympathetic host national:* This is probably a first choice over consistently being with other international students who are in the same boat as you. However, both experiences have an important place, and sometimes the concept of finding a "sympathetic host national" is not easy at all.

*Avoid overly romanticizing* life back home or overly disparaging your host country and its culture. Actively "choose" to stay in a positive frame of mind.

*continued...*

*Gather information:* Read and research about the host country's history, culture, social norms, and politics prior to arrival and during your stay.

*Take a break:* Take a day off to escape or play and do something typically Canadian!

*Maintain contact with friends and family back home:* This connection will help you process and understand your experience as well as provide you with some support. Plus, it will keep your friends and folks from wondering and worrying too much. Be cautious, however, about alarming your relatives about situations they cannot understand or act on.

*Take on challenges you can handle, but don't overdo it:* While getting involved may be your route to a greater understanding of the culture, be careful to know your limits, and know when to say "no."

*Keep a journal:* This is an important space to process your thoughts and experiences and to look back and reflect on the changes you are going through. Have you ever heard of anyone regretting keeping a journal?

*Keep a sense of perspective:* Remember your stay overseas is going to be limited. And trust in your ability to work out problems and find solutions. It might not happen right away but in the long term your challenges will be your greatest asset.

Partially adapted from Hachey (1988; 1998; 2012).

Another useful sight is: Nancy Westfall de Gurolla http://ww2.odu.edu/ao/oip/studyabroad/resourc es/culturaladjustment.pdf

# Safety Issues during Exchange Overseas

## Registration with Canadian consulate

Students must register with the Canadian Consulate/High Commission/Embassy on arrival in the country. If you are not a Canadian, please register in your own country's Consulate, as well.

## Law and legal issues

There are no special laws or exemptions for students. You are subject to the laws of the country in which you are residing. You are also bound by the regulations of your agency. Before you travel, familiarize yourself with the laws and any special situations that may be present in your host country. You should make sure you know the location of the nearest Canadian embassy or consulate. These are five legal rules to keep in mind:

1. Incidents that are viewed as minor offences in Canada may result in a jail sentence in another country.
2. In March of 1999, a tourist in Mexico received a one-year jail term for picking up pieces of pottery as souvenirs. The pottery, found at a Mayan site, was over 2,000 years old. There are laws in Mexico that govern the retrieval and removal of ancient artifacts. Ignorance of the law is not considered an excuse.
3. If you are arrested, you need to contact the Canadian Embassy and your University, specifically your academic Sherpa.
4. We can only work within the legal system of the host country.
5. There is little that your University can do to help you if you are arrested for illegal possession or abuse of an illegal substance.

## Drugs and alcohol

Some countries have more lenient laws regarding alcohol than Canada does. In some cases this means a more relaxed attitude towards drugs as well. The Netherlands take a liberal view regarding the use of marijuana and students in parts of Colombia may find they have easier access to cocaine. Excessive use of drugs and alcohol will cloud your judgment and students who overdo consumption could find themselves in trouble with the law or their agency. Also, be aware that beer in many countries can have higher alcohol content than in Canada.

## Travel precautions

### Women

In some countries it is recommended that women do not travel alone. Even in developed western countries, treatment and views of women will vary. Be aware that what we consider harassment might not be considered so in another culture. There is a difference between being in physical danger and being annoyed, frustrated, and angry. You should be familiar with the customs of dress in the country you are visiting. Observe the women in that culture and dress conservatively regardless of where you are. Five ways for women to be safe include:

1. Know your surroundings and carry a map. It is a good idea to plan your route ahead of time.
2. Ask women for directions.
3. Project a confident attitude. Act like you know where you are going even when you are uncertain.
4. Be cautious about making eye contact, it may be considered an invitation.
5. Don't walk with your head down. Be aware and alert.

### Gays and lesbians

Situations in our partner countries vary greatly from Canada – countries vary in terms of how tolerant they are towards gays and lesbians. Gay bashing is a real risk, particularly if you are in a country where you do not understand the language and cannot adequately assess what is going on around you. Gay and lesbian students may find they have to be more discrete while abroad than they are, for instance, in Calgary. For more information consult the following online resources:

- NAFSA: www.indiana.edu/~overseas/lesbigay
- Amnesty International: www.amnesty.org
- Michigan State University: http://studyabroad.isp.msu.edu/forms/glbt.html

## Photography etiquette

You will probably want to take pictures on your travels and we encourage you to do so. Photos of your friends are usually not a problem since you know them and, in some cases, have their permission. Other kinds of pictures, ones that reflect your experience and impressions of the country may be more problematic. It is important to know that not all cultures regard photography in the way we do in Canada. Taking pictures of people in their own surroundings may be considered intrusive. Many people relate photographs to the exploitation of people during the colonial period. Others may see it as a curse. If you do take pictures of people without their permission, be aware that your actions may provoke hostility. Also, some countries may have restrictions on the buildings, places, and people that you can photograph. For instance, in Ghana, it is illegal to take a picture of some government buildings. Some countries restrict taking pictures in airports. You could be arrested if you do not comply with their regulations.

## Travel safety tips

Inform yourself as much as possible about your host country. Check out the attitudes of local populace towards outsiders. Know the state of the economy, standard of living, and the stability of the government.

## Thirteen general safety precautions

1. Avoid all civil disturbances. Stay in a safe place and keep in touch with the international community and the Canadian embassy.

2. Use a "dummy" wallet or purse and carry $20 or less when walking around town. If you are robbed, give them your dummy wallet.
3. Keep the rest of your money in a safe place and preferably locked.
4. Never flash your money around or have it in a place where people can see it.
5. Notice people around you and your surroundings. Is someone dressed differently or does something seem out of place? If you feel as if something is wrong, you are probably correct.
6. Always walk as if you know what you are doing and have a purpose. If you are unaware of what's going on around you or look confused, you are a soft target and become easy prey.
7. If you are being followed, find a shop or lighted area to go and wait until the person is gone.
8. Beware of scam artists posing as undercover policemen who ask to see your money to determine if it is counterfeit.
9. Do not discuss travel plans with strangers.
10. If you order a canned or bottled liquid, make sure it is unopened when you get it. If it is opened, refuse it.
11. Always carry a card with the phone number of the embassy in case of an emergency.
12. If a local (particularly a taxi driver) gives you a warning, heed that warning. It is wise to crosscheck information, however.
13. Have a communication safety plan, including an international calling card, an international phone number, and embassy number.

## Cultural Etiquette

The more information you know about the host country, city, and community the better prepared you will be in dealing appropriately with any unforeseen difficulties. Do not become complacent, be flexible and keep the whole picture in mind. Follow a code of ethics to help avoid trouble and keep safe during your travels.

The Ecumenical Coalition on Third World Tourism, a non-governmental organization which challenges the negative impacts of tourism on society, offers the following code for travelers.

### Code of Ethics for Travelers — Ecumenical Coalition on Third World Tourism

1. Travel in a spirit of humility and with a genuine desire to learn more about the people of your host country. Be sensitively aware of the feelings of other people, thus preventing what might be offensive behaviour on your part. This applies very much to photography.
2. Cultivate the habit of listening and observing, rather than merely hearing and seeing.
3. Realize that often the people in the country you visit have time concepts and thought patterns different from your own. This does not make them inferior, only different.
4. Instead of looking for the "beach paradise," discover the enrichment of seeing a different way of life, through other eyes.
5. Acquaint yourself with local customs. What is courteous in one country may be quite the reverse in another – people will be happy to help you.
6. Instead of the Western practice of "knowing all the answers," cultivate the habit of asking questions.
7. Remember that you are only one of thousands of tourists visiting this country and do not expect special privileges.
8. If you really want your experience to be a "home away from home," it is foolish to waste money on traveling.
9. When you are shopping, remember that the "bargain" you obtained was possible only because of the low wages paid to the maker.

10. Do not make promises to people in your host country unless you can carry them through.
11. Spend time reflecting on your daily experience in an attempt to deepen your understanding. It has been said, "what enriches you may rob and violate others."

*Source:*    http://resourcepage.gambia.dk/tour_ethics.htm
*Note:*    For further reference concerning cultural etiquette, please refer to the book by Amoja Three Rivers, *Cultural etiquette: A guide for the well-intentioned.*

# Returning Home

All of a sudden, it seems like yesterday that you arrived in your host country, full of anxiety and wonder, to work and study for four months or longer. The culture shock you experienced now seems a distant memory, and you have mixed feelings about going home. Yet returning home can be the most interesting and rewarding part of your journey, if you approach it with the right perspective. Once home, you might notice that you have grown and changed, that your surroundings seem the same but you look at them with different eyes, and that "home" represents a new field of opportunities and challenges. The greatest challenge may be fitting your new self into your old environment. Not everyone will face the same adjustments when returning home. Factors that influence adaptation processes include length of stay, amount of immersion into the culture, your own flexibility, and how much you have kept in contact with your own country and community. Chapter 7 addresses this issue of returning home in more detail.

# Conclusion

Each international exchange has both opportunities and challenges. Making sure that you are sufficiently prepared for this wonderful experience will help reduce the challenges. Understanding what you may experience while on an international exchange and taking safety precautions will help reduce the unhappy experiences as well. Being prepared for your return home will make reintegration into your own country less traumatic. These tips, developed over years of experience, are meant to help you have a happy and fulfilling international exchange.

# Reflection Questions

Please answer the following question before you leave for your host country:

1. What am I expecting to get out of this international experience?
2. What fears do I have regarding this experience?
3. What experiences am I looking forward to having?
4. Am I ready to go?

head home, without telling anyone what had happened. Fortunately, he phoned his academic Sherpa back in Canada, and through her support and guidance, he was able to process the experience and complete his exchange. He also contacted the police, and had enough self-compassion to recognize how this experience would help him to assist traumatized clients.

One young woman became very ill and was overwhelmed by vomiting and diarrhea. She was able to call a new friend who took her to a clinic. She learned how embarrassing it can be to have someone you hardly know translate very personal information.

A young woman from Poland completing her placement in Canada felt disoriented and ill for weeks. Her stoic nature kept her from communicating her difficulties, which made her feel desperate. She eventually saw a doctor and consulted with her local exchange coordinator who helped her to see that her difficulties were partly physical, cultural, and emotional. She had embarked on this journey against her father's wishes and her guilt was at times overwhelming. As she was able to sort through the layers of her distress she started to feel better. She grew to validate her decision and decided to pursue a Masters degree upon her return to Europe, and not return home as her parents had decreed. This was a significant shift for her, and one that required considerable awareness and self-compassion. The opportunity of her exchange intensified her development and gave her the perspective she needed to examine her life.

Anna, a student from Finland who was also in Canada for her exchange, had a similar experience. Her placement was in an emergency shelter for women who had experienced domestic abuse. She didn't know why she felt emotionally fragile and unsettled. As with the second case example, the cause of her troubles turned out to be multi faceted. She was dealing with cultural issues and a sense of isolation, and she began to recognize through her work at the shelter that her father abused her. She suppressed this knowledge for a long time, but in supporting other victims, her own situation became clearer.

Trauma, such as illness, personal revelations, physical and emotional attacks, may be experienced at different levels throughout the international exchange. For many social work and human service students, working with clients can resurrect painful memories. The added intensity of an international exchange can spark change, and forge new understandings that result in life altering awareness, personal growth through trauma and life-changing decisions.

## Facing Cultural Inequalities

Human service students are constantly confronted with the desperate conditions of marginalized populations, regardless of where they work. When faced with beliefs and values that are alien and disturbing, our sense of shock, helplessness and frustration can be almost unbearable. It is critical to bring a sense of balance to the situation. Extreme poverty, filth, different cultural values related to gender, class, religious beliefs and the worth of human life will leave the student stunned. Being non-judgemental, compassionate, and patient are essential qualities to bring to your work anywhere, but particularly to international vocations. Respecting the cultural context and striving to assess the situation from different perspectives can help in understanding the circumstances and can guide you towards solutions or appropriate strategies.

It is often easier to identify structural or organizational difficulties in a new setting, as if they were highlighted against the contrast of home. One student mentioned that he had more opportunities to critically reflect on these issues in his new setting. He also stated that he was sometimes engulfed by feelings of uncertainty, incompetence, and being confronted by the unknown in an unfamiliar environment. On the other hand, he commented that being forced to interact with a wider range of people and circumstances eventually built his confidence. In their research on students who had a field experience in Mexico, Grant and Larson (2006) comment on how students were able to comprehend the structural issues faced by Canadian Aboriginals more clearly after being confronted by inequalities in Mexican society.

The following case study highlights some of the above issues. Spend a few moments reflecting on the questions after the case study.

## A Case Study from India

### The event

> There were so many "beggars" incidents that it is hard to pinpoint one. Last week M__ and I were walking back to our hostel and I saw in the distance a mother with her two children sitting in the median. She noticed us walking and directed her children to approach us. She had a boy (12-years-old) and a girl (6-years-old), both ready to run across the street through traffic, but luckily the mother held them back long enough for the traffic to calm down. I happened to be eating a bag of chips while walking. Both children approached me for money. I declined to give them money; the boy persisted a little more but eventually left us alone, meanwhile, the young girl held on to my shirt and my bag of chips begging for money and chips. She stayed with me for a few minutes until I raised my voice and she ran back to her mother.

*Reflection*

> It is way easier to ignore older beggars than children. Depriving a child of food, who does that? I guess I did. I dislike myself for it. I was shocked to see a mother deliberately send her children after us. Parents should be providing for the child, not the other way around. I was scared for the children. The children were more focused on approaching us than they were of the dense traffic. I was frustrated by how aggressive the girl was as well. I felt really torn between giving and not giving. I could easily afford whatever they were asking. Part of me wanted to give and the other part did not. I felt very confused and angry with myself. Aspects of self that could have contributed to these children approaching me were definitely my race, class, gender, being able bodied, and language (could not speak Marathi and Hindi). All these factors pointed to someone being able and willing to provide to "beggars."

*Questions*

What is your emotional reaction to this incident? Based on your current assessment of yourself, how do you think you might react in a similar situation? How would you reconcile yourself to the social justice issues inherent in this episode? How do you think you would be able to deal with such interactions occurring on a daily basis?

# Relationships

Developing new friendships is an important benefit of international experience. A friend can help you to adjust to living in a different culture. The emotional benefits of having someone to turn to when you feel lonely, frustrated, or elated by some event cannot be under estimated. Relationships can go both ways. On one hand, you may need this relationship more than the other person. On the other hand, the other person may see a relationship with a foreigner as a possible way to escape their living situation or a way out of their country. Nevertheless, many students maintain ongoing contact with friends they made during their exchange. For example, after one young woman returned home, she continued to develop a relationship that she had with a young man. Later, she joined him and his family on a holiday, and a couple of years later they married. She wisely took her time to make certain this was a relationship built on a firm foundation and not one limited by needs of insecurity, fear or gratitude, or fed by lack of perspective. If you are attracted to someone be cautious, maintain your boundaries, stand away from the situation for a time, and be aware of consequences that may ensue in terms of losing accommodation, offending cultural standards, and green card issues.

## Sexual Harassment

Sexual harassment is any unwanted sexual attention including leering, pinching, patting, repeated comments, subtle suggestions of a sexual nature and pressure for dates. It can also take the form of attempted or actual rape. Every culture has different ways of defining appropriate and inappropriate sexual behaviour and it is important to be acquainted with the norms of the host country. Possible sexual harassment situations are as follows:

1. physical assault (including, but not limited to, rape)
2. inappropriate personal questions
3. sexual remarks
4. unwanted touching

Plan your wardrobe, your interactions, and your lifestyle accordingly. Restrictive attitudes towards women exist in many societies. A woman without a male partner may be seen as brazen and daring; harass-

*Ten Tips to prevent sexual harassment:*

1. If you are single, buy a cheap gold ring and wear it.
2. Within reason, follow local rules for male and female interaction.
3. Dress conservatively; follow the local dress code.
4. Appear purposeful and confident.
5. Avoid eye contact with strangers.
6. Think ahead to avoid compromising situations.
7. Remain close to other women in public places.
8. Avoid isolated areas and going out at night alone.
9. Follow your intuition – remove yourself from any situation that does not feel right.
10. Make sure your living accommodation is secure.

*Seven strategies for handling sexual harassment:*

1. Be assertive.
2. Say no and ask the person to leave.
3. Shout or yell; learn an abusive local phrase to shame the man.
4. Find refuge in a store or a group.
5. Ask a local woman for help.
6. In a Muslim country, pull a headscarf partially over your face and turn the other way.
7. Consider taking a self defense course before departure.

ment may be an assertion of male authority or rejection of the "liberated" Western woman. On the other hand, a woman with a male partner may be ignored in his presence. The risk of rape and physical violence varies from society to society and city to city. The perpetrators may be local or expatriate men. If you are raped, you need to seek medical and police help; if possible, have a person you feel comfortable with accompany you. Men are not immune to harassment and should also strive to understand the cultural mores concerning heterosexual and homosexual interactions.

Since societies have different definitions of sexual harassment, you should be aware that complaints might be ignored or looked upon unfavourably. In general, sexual harassment is behaviour that is unwanted and uninvited. It usually, but not always, involves a person with power or authority using that position to coerce sexual relations or to punish refusal. Your university will certainly view this issue seriously, but students are bound by the regulations and procedures in their host country and agency. Universities are very limited in what they can do if a student is a victim of sexual harassment while abroad. If you feel uncomfortable in a situation, or become the recipient of unwanted advances, seek advice from your field instructor.

If you are attacked, seek the advice of your agency and field instructor before calling the police. In some countries, the police system is quite corrupt so you should have your local contacts escort you to the appropriate officials before proceeding with any legal matters.

## General Cultural Challenges

Living and working in another country presents layers of complexity, and it is necessary to acknowledge that you can only partially prepare yourself for this actuality.

### Everyday challenges

One student was taken aback by how much his body reacted to his environment, and it is worth noting that factors such as humidity, heat, weather, stimulation (i.e., colours, smells, and noise) can assault the senses. One young man was not prepared for the number of people smoking in an Austrian agency and had to change his exchange setting because of his body's allergic reaction to smoke.

Different modes of transportation, new routines, and diverse lifestyles can all be unsettling. One young woman was amazed at seeing a Catholic church on seemingly every corner in Poland, and although she had read about the importance of the Catholic religion to the Polish people, it was very different to experience its influence in all aspects of life. The student writes:

> Fish Fridays – it is a Catholic thing. The funny thing is here, if someone asks me if I am Catholic, and I say no, the very next thing they ask is if I am an atheist. It is quite funny because several people have done this. Here, it is like you are either one or the other. Ninety-five percent of the population here is Catholic.

Maki was raised in Japan, immigrated to Canada as a child, and went to India to complete her field placement. She became aware that cultural expectations were affecting her reactions to others. She was raised to value the opinions of those who were humble and modest and was offended by those who acted in a superior fashion. It was her experience in India that highlighted this tendency for her, one that likely had been present in Canada, but was intensified in these new surroundings. She was also reminded of her younger self, who reacted with some fear when she first arrived in Canada and declined opportunities to take risks, and found that she was repeating this reaction in Delhi. She writes:

> Today has been very frustrating. I walked to the Kefirek (grocery store) and got everything I needed. My 50 zl. bill got stuck in my change
>
> *continued...*

purse and a tiny piece of the bill ripped off. The cashier refused to accept it and my debit card wouldn't work. I had an English speaking customer tell her I would go to the bank machine and to keep my groceries for me. I was very upset I had to walk in the freezing cold and snow to the bank machine. I returned in 5 minutes only to find they had put my groceries away. I had to go back and get everything again.

### Another student's voice from India

It was relatively easy to get a prepaid SIM card and phone account set up, all I had to do was provide 2 copies of all my documents along with 2 extra passport size photos; 300 rupees later, I had an Indian mobile number and life was good!

Two days later, I went to make a phone call and it said "call barred." So I tried to call the customer care centre and after 24 tries, I got through to a representative who told me that my account had been temporarily suspended because my address on the form was fake. I went to the office and was told there were many problems including that my address was too short. She said "in India, our addresses are long. For example, "1, Radha Priya Terraces, Near Pratidnya Mangal Kareley, Near Police Choki, Beside Ice Cream Store, Karvenagar, Pune, India, 41123." "My address is XXX Abergale Drive, St. Catherines, Ontario." "No, that's fake. It's too short. I'm sorry but it has to be longer." "How can make it longer?" "I don't know, but you have to." "So I said fine, you want a long address, I'll give you one." So in the end my address turned out be this: XXX Abergale Drive North East, Near Mac's store, Across the Field,

*continued...*

> Beside Abbeydale Elementary School, St. Catherines, Ontario Canada, North America. And with that they were happy. My phone has worked ever since.

> *A student's voice from Poland*
> There are no fridges provided for students in this building. Some buy mini-fridges and some simply put their perishables in a bag and hang it outside of their window. Apparently, you have to tie the bag up really well or the pigeons will get at your butter.

## Cultural challenges in agency

In any setting a student can anticipate being confronted with issues related to culture, whether they are ethnic, religious, age, socioeconomic, gender, sexual orientation, or other factors. Students completing their training in another country are frequently astounded at how their learning is compounded by their environment. Every student struggles with the continuum of self determination and reducing harm, but how do you learn to address these values in an agency that emphasizes these aspects differently than you were taught, due to a cultural construct? In their reflective papers students frequently commented on how they found that their personal assumptions and beliefs were constantly being challenged, and that they began to question the validity of their previous experiences.

One student discovered that his foundational values concerning nutrition, clothing, and parenting principles were being highlighted, and he had to make some fundamental adjustments. Another noted that she was questioning her home child protection standards because of her encounters in her agency. Another commented on how patients in his hospital placement were being placed together regardless of their psychiatric, addiction, or day surgery needs, based on a philosophy that all problems are intertwined.

## Moving from survival to thriving

In many of the reflective exercises you have completed in this book, you will have come closer to identifying some of your strengths in embarking on an international exchange, as well as facing some aspects of yourself that may add some challenges to such an endeavor. It is important to be honest with yourself in this self-exploration in order to be as prepared as possible, and to recognize that no matter how well you think you are equipped for such an adventure, you will still be surprised at some of your reactions. It is critical to start out with a plan on how to look after yourself in order to both get the most out of the experience, and to come home healthy.

All the self care approaches you have learned to adopt throughout your life, as well as those you have learned in your program, will obviously be useful, but due to the added intensity of an international experience, it is even more important to be diligent in your efforts to look after yourself. (See Appendix 4 for a self-care guide at http://www.desitterpublications.com/sherpa_appendix.html.) The critical importance of self-care is highlighted by a student who commented: "I think it was the fact of being away from everything that was familiar and that I would normally use to help myself cope with the stresses of life." You absolutely need a network of support, both back home and in your new environment. You need to have people to talk to, to help you sort out the layers of meaning, and to help you make decisions that are appropriate and constructive both for you and your clients. One student sent regular lengthy emails to her academic Sherpa back home as she struggled to make sense of her circumstances and her reactions.

Many students were required by their home school to write personal reflections as assignments, which helped them organize their thinking and be able to get some response to this process. Their feedback indicated that they found this very useful. Try to reach out before you start to feel overwhelmed. Reach out to your new friends, supports, academic Sherpa, and friends back home.

It is also vital to try and remain physically healthy; perhaps an obvious statement but one that bears repeating. Try and get enough sleep, eat well, get exercise, drink lots of water, follow the guidelines for food safety in your host country, and take vitamins. A significant aspect of health is to have fun, so look for opportunities to socialize and travel.

Another important survival tip is to be sure to keep your sense of humour. It will help you maintain your perspective and will support your efforts to be compassionate with yourself and others.

## Conclusion

This chapter highlights the life changing experience that an international exchange can have on a student. Exposure to a new culture, facing one's own bias, prejudices, reactions, and inner struggles will challenge a student's perspective and socialization. A sense of balance and openness to different ways of knowing are important attributes to carry to a host country. It is also important to acknowledge that unexpected events will happen and it is at these moments that your balance and perspective are drawn upon. Staying safe and healthy (physically, mentally, emotionally, and spiritually) and maintaining a sense of humour will help you to gain the most from your international experience.

## Reflection Questions

1. How would you react to challenges like extreme poverty, filth, different cultural values related to gender, class, religious beliefs and the worth of human life?
2. What will you need to do to be non-judgemental, compassionate, respectful of the cultural context, and assess situations from different perspectives?

# Chapter 7

## Unpacking the Bags and Shelving the Passport

"I never realized that in returning home I would not be instantly home."
*(Storti, 1997, p. 53)*

## Introduction

If the anticipation and build-up to working overseas is exciting and stressful, then returning home can be just as exciting and full of anticipation. Students, having had new and different experiences, want to share these with their loved ones back home. Stepping off the plane, being met by family and friends and showing the new you are wonderful feelings, and yet the re-entry into one's own culture can be more difficult than expected (Alder, 1981; Black & Gregersen, 1999; Grove, 1989; Rohrlich & Martin, 1991; Storti, 1997; Sussman, 1986). It is often "a complicated and usually difficult experience" (Storti, 1997, p.1) and some find it more difficult than adjusting to their overseas experience. Most organizations and travelers pay little attention to this part of the overseas experience (Levy, 2000). "The problem for many returnees is that while they can readily imagine that moving abroad and adjusting to a foreign culture might be a transition, they see coming home as just a matter of arriving at a certain place on a certain day" (Storti, 1997, p. 54). If not adequately dealt with it can become a reason why people's readjustment is slow, difficult and traumatic (Grove, 1989; Szkudlarek, 2010). The re-entry process affects the person returning and their family and friends. This chapter will provide insight and practical guidelines to make re-entry less traumatic. The common phrase "culture shock and reverse culture shock" implies a dramatic experience when, in many instances, re-entry is a mild experience. Thus, as much as possible we use the phrase "re-entry adaptation" instead of reverse culture shock. Re-entry is a mental, emotional, and physical adjustment and understanding these different elements is important. In order to prepare for re-entry, knowing the re-entry stages will go a long way to making this process less traumatic. "The symptoms of re-entry shock can vary both in type and severity. Some individuals feel virtually no effects, while others may take months or even years to re-adjust and feel better" (Yale, 2012). However long it takes, it is not a sign of weakness but is part of the journey.

## Stages of Re-entry

The W-curve, which is an extension of the U-curve described in Chapter 5, incorporates the experience of returning home. This perspective, developed by Gullahorn & Gullahorn (1963), is based on the assumption that the same stages of culture shock (i.e., honeymoon, culture shock, adaptation, and mastery) would also be experienced when re-entrying one's own country, but with one difference. According to Gaw (2000), Gullahorn and Gullahorn noted that one difference between culture shock and reverse culture shock is "the expectations of the sojourners. Sojourners often expected to return to an unchanged home as unchanged individuals, which was not the case" (p. 86). As with the U curve, there is growing criticism of these re-entry stages (La Brack, 2012; Gaw, 2000; Kealey, 2000), and yet they cannot be dismissed altogether. As Gaw (2000) suggests: "Sojourners experience re-entry in different ways; individuals may experience few, if any, effects of re-entry, while others appear to have problems ranging from a few months to a year or longer" (pg. 84). His study of American college students returning from a study abroad program concluded that students may experience re-entry issues including "depression, alienation, isolation, loneliness, general anxiety, speech anxiety, friendship difficulties, shyness concerns, and feelings of inferiority" (p. 101). He also identified issues concerning "trouble studying, academic performance concerns, concerns about a career match and adjustment to the college environment" (p. 101). Furthermore, a student may not seek help available through counseling and student support services. Here are some student's comments about re-entering their own country after living abroad.

I found myself once again profoundly sad that I was leaving! I missed my new friends, the culture, the food, and the landscapes. Conversely, I was also relieved to be returning home to my familiar life, my family and my friends. I found myself confused as I moved in between these opposing feelings. I found that I listened intently to the French radio station whenever I could – I really missed the language. This brought back many memories of being in Belgium and was comforting to me immediately after returning home.

Another student comments on returning home.

Adjusting to coming home was really hard. I felt in some ways that I'd missed out on making connections with local potential employers, given that I'd been out of the country for my fourth year field placement. I also lost touch with a lot of my classmates and maybe didn't get as rich of a student experience as I would have participating in classroom discussions. However, I also had experiences that were so amazing and unique to being abroad that had changed me and taught me so

continued...

much; it was an incredible time of self-discovery which I don't think I would have got at home. I was actually dreading returning home because my relationships had fallen apart, and I knew I'd have to face that, along with finding a job and moving. I returned and quickly became a single, homeless, unemployed student! Looking back it was pretty overwhelming but also quite exciting. It was a lot to take in all at once after being away for so long. Also, I found people would ask about my trip but maybe weren't all that interested. Some people were great but I guess there were others where it felt like they just didn't get me anymore.

## More about Stages of Re-entry

Generally speaking, the re-entry process is comprised of four stages, much like the W-curve. It is important to note that this is a normal process, usually temporary, and is experienced by people differently according to many factors including: 1) how long they have been away; 2) degree of interaction with the host community; 3) a more familiar re-entry environment; 4) amount of interaction with family, friends, and colleagues while away; 5) attitudes of home-country individuals towards returnees; 6) housing conditions at home; and 5) their own preparation for returning home (Storti, 1997; Szkudlarek, 2010).

### Stage one — Leave taking and departure

Say good-bye to friends and colleagues in a culturally appropriate way. Visit places of interest before leaving the country. It is a time to begin to disengage and think about returning home.

### Stage two — Excitement of being home

A wonderful period when everyone is glad to see you and interested in hearing your stories. Eating foods missed while away and doing things you couldn't do in your host country feels like utopia. It's a little like a vacation. This honeymoon period can last from a couple of days to a month depending on many factors.

## Stage three — Difficulties in adaptation

After the excitement of seeing friends and family, experiencing all the good things about home, a low period often follows. Most people think you have settled in quite well and people "more or less leave you to your own devices and at a time when you may be suffering the most, everyone assumes you are fine (Storti, 1997, p. 59). Common experiences during this time are: 1) increased negative judgments about one's own country; 2) the feeling of living in two different worlds; 3) missing the attention of being a foreigner to being anonymous; 4) doubt about whether it was the right decision to return home; 5) being overwhelmed with the many tasks to be done; and 6) an alienation with friends and family. Escape and withdrawal are two common reactions associated with reverse adaptation.

## Stage four — Recovery/Readjustment

The highs and lows of re-entry eventually taper off to a readjustment period. You are feeling safer, trust has been re-established and the focus is now on the

future. A more balanced view of the whole experience is obtained and you are "able to see both home and the host country for what they are and no longer curse the former for not being the later" (p. 65). You are feeling at home again.

These different stages are not necessarily experienced one after the other but they may be experienced at different times in the re-entry process. La Brack (2012) and Szkudlarek (2010) caution using these simplistic models as absolute truth and to be cautious of misleading students on their accuracy. Some of the issues that may occur during these stages can be of a personal and professional level.

## Personal Side of Re-entry

Personal issues will arise when returning home including criticizing your country, sharing your experiences, dealing with serious relationships, missing life abroad, returning to family and communication.

1. ***Criticizing and/or appreciating your own culture and country****.* One of the temptations of a student when returning home is to criticize it. On the other hand, students come back really appreciating their own country. An HRSDC (2009) student reflects on this: "I have a greater appreciation for my family for my health and for my life. I am able to live here in Canada." Criticizing and appreciating one's own country in a constructive and reflective way can be beneficial to the returning student and their friends and family.

2. ***Sharing your experience with others****.* It is important to share your stories with your family and friends. This can be done throughout the overseas experience via email and telephone conversations. Once back home and the pictures are downloaded and the trip has been recorded, inviting family and friends over for a show can be a wonderful way to share the returnee's experience. Be aware that friends and family tire of hearing comparisons

between countries as well as the experience as a whole (Levy, 2000).

3. ***Relationships from the experience***. Long-term serious relationships can develop from an overseas experience. Although this is a great experience, you should be cautious before leaping into a marriage. It is important that you go home as planned, spend time away from that person and readjust and then bring that person over to your country for a visit. It is advisable for both partners in a relationship to take time to think through each other's cultures and how marriage will work in this context.

4. ***Things that you will miss or not miss about your host country***. Missing daily activities, conversing with friends, and experiencing new adventures in the host country are common. Life back home can be boring and difficult. It is also common to not miss certain activities, friends and adventures. The lack of resources, irritating cultural habits, taking twice as long to get anything accomplished, getting robbed, and dealing with health issues are several of the many things that students will not miss.

5. ***Returning to live with family***. Adjusting to family life can be difficult as well, not just for the student, but also for the partner or parents. Taking time to adjust and communicating thoughts and feelings are key to dealing with these issues.

6. ***Maintaining communication***. The Internet and email can positively affect the re-entry process. Communication throughout the time abroad can keep your family and friends up-to-date on what you are experiencing and learning and vice versa (Adler, 1981; Levy, 2000). Also, once you return home, you can continue communicating with the friends and colleagues in the host country.

## Professional Side to Adjustment

Professional issues will arise when returning home. They include opportunities to share your experience with colleagues, using the experience to gain employment, and contributing to your community.

1. ***Debriefing with instructors***. During the initial re-entry stages, a debriefing with the academic sherpa of the program is important. This helps to iron out any difficulties, complaints, joys, excitement of the experience and gives grounding to the re-entry process. This can be an informal process or in the form of an exit interview. It can also be in the form of a re-entry workshop (Grove, 1989; Sussman, 1986). However it is done, you need the time and attention from the academic sherpa to work through your experience.

2. ***Preparing and giving presentations***. You can use the overseas experience to help you professionally, by preparing and giving presentations concerning your experience overseas.

3. ***Using the experience for career purposes***. One student said that "International experience is a huge asset in the professional world. Becoming more confident in a second language is also key."

   There are mixed messages out in the community as to how important an overseas experience can be to professional development (Adler, 1981; Westwood et al., 1986; Szukudlarek, 2010). Nevertheless, you will have learned useful knowledge and skills that you can present to potential employers (Adler, 1981; Black & Gregersen, 1999). Your understanding of cultural differences may be an asset in the work place. Three important skills acquired by the HRSDC Canadian students were: 1) intercultural understanding; 2) ability to work in a multicultural environment; and 3) self-confidence and initiative. The three most important skills acquired by the HRSDC European students were 1) critical thinking; 2) openness; and 3) ability to work in a multicultural environment. Colleagues will notice a person with a broad view of work and life. If a student is interested in working as an international social worker, this experience will help in acquiring the right job and should be highlighted in interviews. The following students view their overseas experience as helping them to gain employment at home:

### Student 1

To this day I still believe that my international Masters in Social Work placement in Belgium landed me my pivotal professional career position as the executive director of a coalition to end violence against women.

### Student 2

Being involved in an international field placement directly impacted my ability to secure full-time employment. I enjoyed working in Finland so much that when I returned home I chose to pursue a career in child welfare. My supervisors in Finland provided references attesting to my field placement experience and I was able to secure full-time employment with a child welfare organization in Canada.

4. ***Using your experience to contribute to your own community, province, and country***. Apart from the college or university, opportunities are available for students to share their experience in the community, province, and country. Locally, students can set up a time to speak at a public meeting in the community, either through a community centre or through the organization that sent them in the first place. They can be involved in organizations that are committed to social justice issues around the world. At the provincial level, conferences offer opportunities for people to share their experience. Writing an article is another way to share experiences.

5. ***Evaluation of the experience***. A most important aspect of the whole overseas experience is preparing a good evaluation process so that the organizational aspects of the program can improve. This evaluation process can include exit interviews, survey interviews, and focus groups. The evaluation process helps students through re-entry and helps them to conceptualize and integrate their overseas experience into their own personality and life in the future.

6. ***Institutional support to re-entering students.*** One of the major criticisms of the overseas experience is the lack of time given by organizations in helping people deal with the emotional, psychological, and physical issues around re-entering their own country (Levy, 2000; Stroh, Gregersen, & Black, 1998). The debriefing process is often too soon, short, and superficial. The institution can do several things to help the re-entry process including: 1) providing opportunities for students to share their experience; 2) providing debriefing time; 3) providing time to help students identify skills and knowledge they acquired overseas; and 4) to use them as consultants for students who are just beginning the process. Tange (2005) suggests that a planned re-integration process, by setting up different phases of re-entry, is necessary, particularly when coming back to an employment situation that one had before going overseas.

## Activities to do to Make Re-entry Less Traumatic

The following is a list of activities for students when they finish their overseas experience. These 14 tips will make the re-entry process less traumatic.

1. Have a good departure from the host country, saying good-bye to friends and colleagues and seeing things you wanted to see in that country. Tie up any loose ends before leaving. Give gifts when appropriate.

2.  Read about issues surrounding re-entry and ask the following questions: 1) what are my assumptions and expectations on coming home? 2) Do I accept that I will not be the same as when I left, and my friends and family will have changed? 3) How can I make my re-entry less traumatic?

3.  Give yourself time and personal attention through this re-entry process. Get plenty of rest and take your time re-orientating your body to different foods and environment.

4.  Avoid making any major decisions about your life for the first few months of re-entry.

5.  Be patient with people in your own country that seem narrow minded, wasteful, and superficial. Use your criticism in a constructive way through your own example of living and through participating in educational avenues provided by the community.

6.  When first arriving home, focus on and prioritize each practical task one at a time to avoid being overwhelmed. Before you know it, you will have accomplished a lot.

7.  Share your experience with your family and friends. Remember that your friends and family have a short attention span. When telling your story, always ask what your listeners have gone through during your absence and this will help in keeping the relationship more balanced.

8.  Keep a journal of your first six months back home.

9.  Tensions and problems that you left behind while overseas will come back to you eventually. Be honest with yourself and deal with these when they arise.

10. Talk to your academic sherpa and colleagues at the University about your experience. Identify skills and knowledge acquired through the experience.

11. Present in a class and in the community about your experience. Give the positives of going overseas as well as the not so positive side of the experience.

12. Get involved in community projects that use the skills, knowledge, and expertise you gained from your experience.

13. Find other people in your community who have been to the host country and seek out their friendship and support.
14. Keep in contact with your friends and colleagues in your host country and invite them to come and visit you. If you or the other person wants to stay in touch, then both will make the effort to do so.

## Conclusion

Coming home from an international experience is not always easy. This chapter identified possible issues a student will face when returning home and provides suggestions to make this adjustment easier. Below is a reflective exercise that will help identify feelings and thoughts concerning your transition back home.

## Reflection Questions

The following questionnaire is adapted from the Newcomer's Guide website called "Culture shock and reverse culture shock" available at http://newcomers-guide.mit.edu/ng/culture-shock.

Just before leaving your host country, answer the following items to help you reflect on your experience:

1. Five things that I have enjoyed **most** about living abroad are:
2. Five difficulties that challenged me the **most** while living abroad are:
3. Five things I missed **most** about home while I was away are:
4. The five things (people, places, and activites in my home country) I missed **least** since being away are:
5. My greatest single challenge while living abroad was:
6. My greatest single challenge when returning home will be:

On your return home, approximately two weeks after you return, answer the following questions:

1. Five things I have enjoyed **most** about being home are:
2. Five things that bother me **most** about being home are:
3. Five international things (people, places, and situations) I miss the **least** since returning home are:
4. The five things (people, places, and activities) I miss the **most** from the host country since returning home are:
5. My greatest single challenge since returning home is:

Now compare the two lists and with the help of your institution, share these reflections with other students who have been abroad, as well as with your family, friends, and colleagues.

There is a vast amount of material online concerning re-entry using Google. For more in-depth re-entry orientations, voluntary organizations like VSO/CUSO can help. Grove (1989) and Sussman (1986) provide more in-depth, re-entry orientation ideas.

# Chapter 8

## Conclusion

The Sherpa has taken you down the mountain safely and you return home after an amazing international experience. You will reflect on what you learned during this journey many times throughout your life.

There are numerous themes that recur in this manual. We will touch on each of them briefly to remind you of the most important ideas to support you in your international exchange.

## Eight Key Themes in My Backpack

### 1. Globalization

There is a growing interest in the internationalization of human service professions (especially social work), education, scholarship, and practice as we shift towards a global society. We are more aware today of the global impact of economic, social, political, and cultural problems, and the link between local problems to global issues. In this context, social workers need to be more effective players in responding to the realities of global interdependency (Ife, 2007). There is a move to provide students with attributes and skills required in international exchanges, and curriculum content in many schools is drawing more attention to developing a critical analysis of world context.

### 2. Anti-oppressive practice (AOP)

Humility and non-judgment are the most important attitudes to take to any international exchange.

Going to a host country with an open mind and an open attitude to reciprocity can make or break an internship. Understanding your own social location before going abroad will help to prepare for the unexpected challenges of racism and oppression that may be experienced or that others will experience by you. We are both the oppressor and the oppressed and understanding these possible actions will help us act in a more anti-oppressive way.

## 3. Finding an exchange

Many of the skills that you would use to find a job can be applied to finding an exchange program. Think about your interests, skills, and previous experiences in deciding what kind of exchange would best suit your needs, and what kind of organization would fit your learning style. Produce a resume that highlights the experiences that would make you attractive to an organization in the field in which you are interested.

## 4. Academic and agency Sherpas

There will be people who will help you arrange for and organize your international experience. Your academic Sherpa may engage in numerous roles such as negotiator, educator, administrator, cultural guide, information conduit, risk manager, problem solver, counselor, and diplomat. It is helpful to understand these roles and how your Sherpa can assist you.

## 5. Learning goals

One of your first activities is to establish what it is that you want to learn during your international exchange. All schools of social work, as well as other human service professions, have learning goals and related activities for international exchanges that offer a structured learning experience. These activities will enable you to learn about the country that you will be traveling to and become educationally prepared for the exchange. But one of your primary learning goals, which should be initiated as soon as you decide to engage in an international exchange, is to learn the language of your host country.

## 6. Preparation

Preparing for an international exchange can be time consuming and should start once it is clear that the exchange is taking place. Not only does it require early planning, it also requires making sure that family and friends are aware of the exchange and that appropriate arrangements are made regarding your job, relationships, and other commitments that need to be addressed. Understanding what you may experience while on an international exchange and taking safety precautions will help reduce unwanted experiences. Being prepared for your return home will make reintegration into your own country less traumatic.

## 7. Open minded

A sense of balance and openness to different ways of knowing are important attributes to carry to a host country, as well as an understanding that as much as one can prepare for all types of situations, unexpected events occur, and it is at these moments when you can draw on your balance and perspective. Keeping yourself safe and healthy physically, mentally, emotionally, and spiritually is important and being gentle with yourself and maintaining a sense of humour will help you through challenging moments, and to move from surviving to thriving.

## 8. Re-entry

Returning home can be just as exciting and full of anticipation as preparing to work overseas. You will want to share your experiences with your loved ones back home. Stepping off the plane, being met by family and friends and showing the new you are wonderful feelings, yet the re-entry into your culture can be more difficult than expected. Knowing the stages of re-entry that you will experience and knowing that your experiences are normal will help make returning much easier.

In conclusion, we share this one last quote from a student who engaged in an exchange in Belgium:

I am learning so much during my stay here. I am super thankful for this experience – it's amazing. My French skills are getting better every week. E__ has refused to speak English with me when we are together (unless we are talking about something serious), and I find myself saying "what" less and less, which is a good feeling. My field placement has also been going really well. It took me a while to get over the shock of it being so incredibly different. I still have to tell myself to relax and just take it in sometime, instead of trying to understand and frame everything from the knowledge of my cultures. I have learned to relax in the midst of feeling that things are uncertain, unfamiliar, and undefined – a huge step for me. My placement has been fruitful not only in terms of what it has taught me about European culture, but also about my own culture. I have been lucky enough to have the privilege of learning about two cultures during my stay here. To say the least, it has been an incredible learning experience that has opened my mind and widened my views on a lot of things. It's been great.

# Appendicies

## APPENDIX 1

### Memorandum of Understanding (MOU)
### University/Field Agency Agreement

_____

_____

_____

(hereinafter called the "Agency")

of the FIRST PART

AND:

### THE GOVERNORS OF THE UNIVERSITY OF HOME UNIVERSITY
a corporation created pursuant to
The Universities Act, R.S.A. 1980, Chapter U-5

of the SECOND PART

WHEREAS the Faculty of Social Work of the University wishes to use the facilities of the Agency for the education of students, for the conduct of social work research and for the continued opportunity for practice of social work by the Social Work faculty;

AND WHEREAS the Agency has agreed to participate in the education of students by providing opportunities as set out in the Field Practicum Manual, the conduct of social work research and the continued opportunity for practice by Social Work faculty.

THEREFORE, in consideration of the mutual promises and covenants contained herein, the sufficiency of which is acknowledged, the parties agree that:

## DEFINITIONS

In this Agreement, the following words and phrases shall have the following meanings:

a)   "**Confidential Information**" means all information which is of a confidential or secret nature, now or hereafter existing, which may be related to the business and management of either party or the personal information of the Student to which access is granted or obtained by the other party, but does not include information which

  (i)   was known to the recipient prior to the disclosure to it by the other party;
  (ii)  was independently developed by the recipient as evidenced by records;
  (iii) is subsequently lawfully obtained by the recipient from a third party;
  (iv)  becomes publicly available other than through breach of this Agreement;
  (v)   is disclosed where the other party has provided its prior written consent; or
  (vi)  is disclosed by legal requirement;

b)   "**Delegate**" means that person designated or appointed by the Agency to be responsible for carrying out the terms of this Agreement on behalf of the Agency;

c)   "**Faculty**" means one or more academic staff, both full-time faculty and sessional instructors of the University who may be involved in a Practicum at the Agency;

d)   "**FOIP**" means *Freedom of Information and Protection of Privacy Act*, S.A. 1994, c-F-18.5, as amended;

e) "**Student**" means a student enrolled in undergraduate or graduate studies in the Faculty of Social Work at the University;

f) "**Practicum**" means (i) a supervised learning opportunity at the Agency for the Student to develop knowledge, skills and attitudes related to professional social work as set out in the MSW Field Practicum Manual; (ii) continued opportunity for the practice of social work by the Faculty; or (iii) for the conduct of research by students or faculty, and in accordance with requirements established by the University;

g) "**Field Instructor**" means a professional Social Worker employed by or contracted to the Agency, registered in accordance with the standards established by the professional association to which the Social Worker is accountable, who has agreed to provide supervision to the Student or any other professional accepted by the University to provide supervision to the Student;

h) "**University**" means the University of Calgary and, in particular, the Faculty of Social Work at the University of Calgary.

## ARTICLE 1
## PRACTICUM PARTICIPATION

1.1 It is mutually agreed that the services provided by the Agency may be utilized by the Student or Faculty for a Practicum or research in agreed upon areas of the Agency, with such areas to be available to the Student and the Faculty at the times arranged by the Dean of the Faculty of Social Work or her/his designate in consultation with the Delegate of the Agency.

1.2 The University and the Agency shall mutually agree upon the particulars of the Practicum. The Student and/or Faculty shall attend at the Agency at times designated by the Agency and agreed to by the University.

1.3 The Agency acknowledges that, during the Practicum, a Student or Faculty may use the facilities, resources and services of the Agency in accordance with the policies, rules, regulations and procedures of the Agency.

1.4 In developing plans for the Practicum, the University will make the arrangements with the Delegate of the Agency.

1.5 The Agency will, in consultation with the University, determine the number of students that can be effectively accommodated at the Agency.

1.6 The Practicum may include social work research projects which will be conducted by the Student or Faculty in conjunction with the Agency adhering to the guidelines and policies of ethics review with human subjects.

1.7 The Agency and the Faculty shall cooperate in the evaluation of the Student during the Practicum.

## ARTICLE 2
## TERM

2.1 The Agreement shall commence September, 2002 and shall continue in force until _____, 200_, at which time it may be renewed by mutual agreement of the parties, subject to termination in clause 5.4.

## ARTICLE 3
## RESPONSIBILITIES OF THE UNIVERSITY

3.1 The University shall ensure that its Student and Faculty are made aware of the policies, rules and regulations of the Agency and the University will take reasonable steps to see that they comply.

3.2 The University shall provide the Agency with the University's policies, rules and regulations which are necessary for the Agency to effectively and safely participate in the Practicum.

3.3 The parties agree that the Student shall sign a Confidentiality Agreement with the University prior to the Practicum.

3.4 The University acknowledges that it has worker's compensation coverage for the Student during the term of the Practicum.

3.5 The Faculty will interpret the Student's educational programs to a Delegate and will receive advice from the Delegate.

3.6 The Student or Faculty shall undertake Practicum activities at the Agency in such a manner that shall result in the least amount of interruption to the Agency and its clients.

3.7 The University and Faculty will collaborate with the Agency to assure adequate guidance of Students to a standard that is based on the well being of the Agency, its clients and professional social work standards.

3.8 The Faculty, in liaison with the Agency, will provide supervision and instruction to the Student unless other mutually agreeable provisions are made, such as a Preceptor being provided.

3.9 In the event of a field education experience, the Faculty shall collaborate regularly with the Agency to assure reasonable guidance and support in carrying out the educational plan for the Student.

## ARTICLE 4
## RESPONSIBILITIES OF THE AGENCY

4.1 The Agency will provide the Faculty and Student with an orientation to its facilities, administrative structure and policies as necessary for the Faculty and the Student to effectively and safely participate in the Practicum.

4.2 The Agency will ensure that their staffs are made aware of the policies, rules and regulations of the University and that the Agency will take reasonable steps to see they comply.

4.3 The Agency will provide the use of available facilities to the Faculty and the Student such as
   (i)  suitable conference room space on schedules basis;

(ii)  cloak room space; and

(iii) materials and equipment, such as telephones
and facsimile machines;

as reasonably necessary for instructional purpose.

4.4 The Agency agrees to ensure that the Student
receives adequate and appropriate direction by the
Agency to fulfill the Practicum requirements.

4.5 The Agency acknowledges the student status of the
Student and shall not require her or him to undertake
activities, responsibilities or duties that exceed
those appropriate for a Student.

4.6 The Agency may provide evaluation and assessment
to the University as to the Student's performance in
the Practicum in those instances where a Faculty is
actively involved in the Practicum with the Student.

4.7 In those instances in which a Preceptor is involved,
the Agency will ensure that the Preceptor cooperates
with the University in the evaluation and
assessment of the Student's performance in the
Practicum.

4.8 The Agency may provide feedback about the University
program to the University to ensure the Student's
learning experiences are consistent with the
Agency's practices and standards.

4.9 The Agency, at all times, reserves the right to refuse
access to facilities to any Student or Faculty.

**ARTICLE 5**
**GENERAL**

5.1 With respect to University servants, employees or
agents, including the Student, the University agrees
at all times to indemnify the Agency and save it
harmless from all manner of action, case of action,
suit, claim, demand and cost whatsoever arising
from any actions of the Student, servants, employees
or agents of the University done in pursuance of
this Agreement during the Practicum.

5.2 In like fashion, the Agency agrees to indemnify the University and save it harmless from all manner of action, cause of action, suit, claim, and cost whatsoever arising from any actions of servants, employees or agents of the Agency done in pursuance of the Agreement during the Practicum.

5.3 Both parties shall insure their operations under a contract of comprehensive general liability insurance with an insurer licensed in Alberta in the amount of not less than $2,000,000 per occurrence, insuring against bodily injury, personal injury and property damage, including the use thereof. The parties shall provide proof of insurance in the form of a certificate of insurance upon request.

5.4 Either party may give notice to terminate this Agreement without cause, by giving to the other party notice in writing on or before April 1 in any year, such termination to become effective on the July 1 immediately following. Notices shall be forwarded by facsimile or any other electronic transmission to:

If to the Agency:

If to the University:

Dean, SCHOOL of Social Work

5.5 No modification of this Agreement shall be effective unless it refers to this Agreement, is made in writing and is signed by authorized representatives of each party.

5.6 If a provision of this Agreement is wholly or partially unenforceable for any reason, such unenforceability shall not affect the enforceability of the balance of this Agreement, and all provisions of this Agreement shall, if alternative interpretations are applicable, be construed as to preserve the enforceability hereof.

5.7 This constitutes the entire agreement between the parties and supersedes all other agreements between the parties.

5.8   The Agency and University acknowledge that the Student is not an employee, independent contractor or agent of the Agency during the term of the Practicum.

5.9   The Agency and University agree that copyright and all other intellectual property rights in the Practicum are and remain the property of the University subject to its intellectual property policy, and that all materials and supplies furnished or provided by the University for use in the performance of this Agreement, do not become the property of the Agency.

5.10  Any word herein contained importing the singular number shall include the plural and vice versa and any word importing the masculine gender shall include the feminine gender and vice versa wherever the context so requires.

## ARTICLE 6

**FREEDOM OF INFORMATION**

6.1  The parties acknowledge that they are both subject to the FOIP. All of the terms and conditions of this Agreement shall be carried out in compliance with the FOIP, and where there are any inconsistencies between this Agreement and the FOIP, the FOIP shall govern.

6.2  The University shall use reasonable efforts to ensure that the Student and Faculty involved with Agency staff, are aware of the obligations of the Agency pursuant to the FOIP, and shall comply with those obligations.

6.3  Subject to FOIP, each party agrees not to disclose Confidential Information and without affecting the generality of the foregoing, Agency specifically agrees that any Confidential Information of the Student or Faculty obtained by Agency shall only be used by Agency for purposes reasonably associated with the Practicum.

IN WITNESS WHEREOF, the parties or their authorized representatives have duly executed this Agreement as of the day and year first above written.

**ON BEHALF OF THE AGENCY:**

_____

_____
Date

**ON BEHALF OF THE GOVERNORS
OF THE UNIVERSITY OF CALGARY:**

_____
Dean, Faculty of Social Work

_____
Date

## APPENDIX 2

## Example Timetable for Academic Sherpa

(This assumes that the exchange is taking place in the Fall term- adjust it if the exchange timing is different).

### July/August:
Incoming students:

- Receive information about incoming students
- Find new placement or contact standing placement for international students
- Coordinate accommodations (may just mean checking that students have arranged housing

Outgoing students:

- Meet with outgoing students
- Check to see if they have the proper documentation (i.e., visa), plane tickets
- Complete pre-trip evaluation forms, initial reimbursement paperwork, if applicable
- Review learning contract

### September:
Incoming Students:

- Receive incoming students, make sure that they will be picked up at airport
- Take students to placements for interviews
- Assist with housing, registration, getting an ID, and bus passes

Outgoing Students:

- Send off outgoing students
- Start formalized support- on-line seminar, and on-going journals
- Facilitate course credit if they find unplanned educational opportunities abroad

### October/November:

- Arrange for incoming students to do presentations in classes or special seminars about their home country and social work in their country

**December:**

Incoming Students:

- Communicate with home university about placement performance
- Send appropriate forms to home university

Outgoing students:

- Submit grades and return files and paperwork to appropriate person
- Meet with returning students and collect receipts for reimbursement
- Have students complete evaluations, turn in journals, assignments, and case studies

**January:**

- Arrange for returning outgoing students to do presentation about their experiences

**February/March:**

- Recruitment of new outgoing students and including attending field orientation events if possible
- Prepare annual report for funder

**April:**

- Selection of outgoing students and review application forms
- International Office workshops for outgoing students
- Courses on cultural preparation

**May/June:**

Writing/dissemination/conference presentations

## APPENDIX 3

### Sample: Guidelines for International Placements

The School of Social Work is open to the establishment of international placements; however these decisions are made in the context of limited resources. Out of country placements can provide enriching experiences for certain students. These placements can provide opportunities for useful comparative studies for students, sometimes enriched by the experience of living in a different setting. It is essential, however, that students are well prepared for the placements and that the practicum coordinator is confident in the student's ability to benefit from a distance educational experience.

Only students who have completed all the prerequisite course work will be considered for a 4th year international practicum.

**A. Criteria for eligibility are based on consideration of the following issues**:

- maturity of student and demonstrated ability to follow-through
- high level of self-direction, initiative, and clarity of purpose
- good level of academic performance (we will obtain a transcript)
- strength of proposal
- quality of student's references
- strong previous placement evaluation if the student did a third year practicum
- appropriate rationale for placement
- learning needs could be better met at a distance than locally
- consideration of financial needs of student and financial issues related to placement
- consideration of a student's future employment possibilities

## B. Agency Criteria

- The placement setting must be committed to meeting the requirements of a placement such as providing the student with appropriate work assignments, with regular supervision and the other requirements as outlined
- Appropriateness of the placement being able to meet objectives of the School of Social Work practicum, including a structural/anti-oppressive perspective
- Commitment of the practicum supervisor to provide one to one and a half hours of supervision per week
- Commitment of the practicum supervisor to meet three times with the faculty liaison
- Willingness of the practicum supervisor to write an evaluation at the end of placement

## C. Student Proposal

Students must develop a practicum proposal, part I of which should be submitted to the practicum coordinator six months in advance of the beginning of the semester in which the student is planning to do her/his placement. Parts II and III should be submitted three months in advance of the beginning of the practicum.

**Part I** (submitted six months in advance)

In this section of the proposal students should address the following:

1) why the student wishes to do an international placement
2) what are the student's learning objectives
3) where is the student wanting to go
4) the names of two SSW faculty who would be prepared to be verbal references

**Part II** (submitted three months in advance)

In this section students should provide the following:

5) an outline of a possible placement detailing the placement opportunities

6) additional information about the setting that will help the academic Sherpa understand the learning opportunity
7) an outline how this placement will meet the student's learning objectives
8) who would supervise the student and her or his credentials (preferably a copy of their resume)
9) suggestions for how the field seminar expectations might be met if an online chat seminar is not available
10) while the academic Sherpa is responsible for assigning a faculty liaison, identify any suggestions of who might be available to act as faculty liaison (consider schools of social work in the community)

**Part III** (submitted three months in advance)

This section is only required for international placement.

11) identify what cultural and international orientation the student will participate in prior to departure in order to prepare for the cultural differences and who will provide this orientation. (Carleton University International Student Services Office provides a one day orientation in early April each year.)
12) address the issue of reciprocity given possible language limitations, the historical context of social work in that country, and how to make a contribution in a culturally meaningful manner
13) address how the student will finance this experience. The school does not have the institutional means to help students finance an international placement. It is the responsibility of the student to explore financial options
14) provide a risk assessment (safety concerns) of the environment where the student will be working
15) address how an aspect of this experience will be presented to the school community, if feasible
16) address health and insurance coverage
17) sign a University Assumption of Risks, Responsibility and Liability Waiver

# References

Alder, N.J. (1981). Re-entry: Managing cross-cultural transitions. *Group and organization management, 6,* 341-356.

Amnesty International. (2012). Learning about human rights. London: Amnesty International. Retreived from http://www.amnesty.org

Asamoah, Y., Healey, L.M., & Mayadas, N. (1997). Ending the international-domestic dichotomy: New approa-ches to a global curriculum for the millennium. *Journal of Social Work Education, 33*(2), 389-401.

Baines, D. (2011). *Doing anti-oppressive practice: Social justice social work*. Halifax: Fernwood Publishing.

Baines, D. (2007). Anti-oppressive social work practice: Fighting for space, fighting for change. In D. Baines (Ed.), *Doing anti-oppressive practice: Building transformative politicized social work*. Halifax: Fernwood Publishing.

Barlow, C.A., (2007). In the third space: A case study of Canadian students in a social work practicum in India. *International Social Work, 50,* 243-254.

Barlow, C.A., & Hall, B. (2007). What about my feelings? A study of emotion and tension in social work field education. *Social Work Education, 26*(4), 399-413.

Barlow, C.A. (2006). An India-Canada field education partnership: Challenges and opportunities. *Indian Journal of Social Work, 67*(1), 36-48.

Barlow, C.A., Schwartz, K., Kreitzer, L., Lacroix, M., Macdonald, L., Lichtmannegger, S., Klassen, M., Orjasniemi, T., & Meunier, D. (2010a). Perspectives of international partners on the development and implementation of a Canada-EU social work field education exchange, *Canadian Social Work Review*, 27(1), 5-25.

Barlow, C.A., Klassen, M., Schwartz, K., Kreitzer, L., Lichtmannegger, S., Lacroix, M., Macdonald, L., Orjasniemi, T., & Meunier, D., (2010b). EU-Canada social work exchange: An EU perspective of opportunities and challenges, Revista de Asistenta Sociala, *Romanian Social Work Review,* 1, 43-57.

Bhabha, H.K. (1994) *The location of culture*. London: Routledge.

Black J.S., & Gregersen, H.B. (1999). The right way to manage expats. *Harvard Business review, March-April.* CUSO VSO (2009). Impactful volunteering. Video available at http://www.cuso-vso.org

Bogo, M. (2006). *Social work practice: Concepts, processes, & interviewing*. New York, NY: Columbia University Press.

Bogo M., & Vayda, E. (2000). *The practice of field instruction in social work: Theory and process* (2nd ed.). New York, NY: Columbia University Press.

Carrol, J., & Ryan, J. (2005). *Teaching international students. Improving learning for all*. New York, NY: Routledge.

Carrol, J. (2005). Strategies for becoming explicit. In J. Carrol & J. Ryan (Eds.), *Teaching international students: Improving learning for all* (pp. 26-35). New York, NY: Routledge.

Chaussain, J.L. (2006). Sur la fiabilité des examens médicaux visant à déterminer l'âge à des fins judiciaires et la possibilité d'amélioration en la matière pour les mineurs étrangers isolés. Academy Nationale de Medecine. Retrieved from http://www.sdj.be/admin/docmena/Avis_ACADEMIE_NATIONALE_DE_MEDECINE__France_.pdf

Conway, J., & Pawar, M. (2005). International social work: Nature, scope, and practice issues. In M. Alston & J. McKinnon (Eds.), *Social work fields of practice* (2nd ed., pp. 268-315). New York, NY: Oxford University Press.

Cox, D., & Pawar, M. (2006). *International social work. Issues, strategies and Programs.* Thousand Oaks, CA: Sage Publication.

Dominelli, L., & Bernard, W.T. (2003). *Broadening horizons: International exchanges in social work.* Aldershot, Hants, England: Ashgate.

Dubois, M., & Ntetu, A. (2000). Learning cultural adaptation through international social work training. *Canadian Social Work,* 2(2).

Elliot, J.A. (1997). Conclusion. In N.S. Mayadas, T.D. Watts, & D. Elliot, (Eds), *International handbook on social work theory and practice* (pp. 441-450). Westport, CT: Greenwood Press.

Ferguson, I., & Lavalette, M. (2006). Globalization and global justice: Towards a social work of resistance. *International social work,* 49(3), 309-318.

Fisher, R., Ury, W., & Patton, B. (1991). *Getting to yes: Negotiating an agreement without giving in* (2nd Ed.). London: Random House.

Freire, P. (1973). *Education for critical consciousness.* New York, NY: Seabury Press.

Freire, P. (1997/1968). *Pedagogy of the oppressed.* New York, NY: The Continuum Publishing Co.

Freire, P. (1998). *Teachers as cultural workers: Letters to those who dare teach.* Boulder, CO: Westview Press.

Furman, R., Coyne, A., & Negi, N.J. (2008). An international experience for social work students. Self-reflection through poetry and journal writing exercises. *Journal of Teaching in Social Work,* 28(1/2), 71-85.

Gammonley, D., Rotabi, K.S., & Gamble, D.N. (2007). Enhancing global understanding with study abroad. Ethically grounded approaches to international learning. *Journal of Teaching in Social Work,* 27 (3/4), 115-135.

Garber, R. (1997). Social work education in an international context. Current trends and future direction. In M.C. Hokenstad & J. Midgley (Eds.), *Issues in international social work. Global challenges for a new century* (pp.159-172). Washington, DC: NASW Press.

Gaw, K.F. (2000). Reverse culture shock in students returning from overseas. *International journal of Intercultural relations, 24,* 83-104.

Gilin, B., & Young, T. (2009). Educational benefits of international experiential learning in an MSW program. *International Social Work,* 52(1), 36-47.

Greulich W.W., & Pyle S.I. (1959). Radiographic atlas of skeletal development of the hand and wrist (Vol. 1). Palo Alto, CA: Stanford University Press.

*Guide on the Asylum Procedure in Belgium* (English Ed.). (2008). Coordination et Initiatives pour et avec Réfugiés et Étrangers. Retrieved from http://www.cire.be

Gullahorn, J.T., & Gullahorn, J.E. (1963). An extension of the U-curve hypothesis. *Journal of Social Issues, 19*(3), 33-47.

HRSDC (2009). *Evaluation of the program.* Calgary, AB: University of Calgary.

Hachey, J-M. (1988). *Canadian guide to living and working overseas.* Ottawa: Intercultural systems and Canadian Bureau for international education.

Hachey, J-M. (1998). *What in the world is going on?* Ottawa, ON: Canadian Bureau for international education.

Hachey, J-M. (2012). *Jean-Marc Hachey.* Retrieved from http://www.workingoverseas.com/hachey

Healy, L., & Link, R.J. (2012). Models of internationalizing curriculum (pp. 329-335). In L. Healy & R. Link (Eds.), *Handbook of international social work.* New York, NY: Oxford University Press.

Healy, L.M. (2001). *International social work: Professional action in an interdependent world.* New York, NY: Oxford University Press.

Healy, L.M. (1986). The international dimension in social work education: Current efforts, future challenges. *International Social Work, 29,* 135-147.

Heron, B. (2005). Changes and challenges. Preparing social work students for practicums in today's sub-Saharan African context. *International social work, 48*(6), 782-793.

Hokenstad, T. (2012). Social work education: The international dimension. In K. Lyons, T. Hokenstad, M. Pawar, N. Huegler, & N. Hall (Eds.), *The Sage handbook of international social work*. Thousand Oaks, CA: Sage Publications.

Hokenstad, M.C., & Midgley, J. (2004). *Issues in international social work. Global challenges for a new century*. Washington, DC: NASW Press.

Hokenstad, M.C., & Midgley, J. (1997). Realities of global interdependence. Challenges for social work in a new century. In M.C. Hokenstad & J. Midgley (Eds.), *Issues in international social work. Global challenges for a new century* (pp.1-10). Washington, DC: NASW Press.

Hokenstad, M.C., Khinduka, S.K., & Midgley, J. (1992). Social work today and tomorrow: An international perspective. In M.C. Hokenstad, S.K. Khinduka, & J. Midgley (Eds.), *Profiles in international social work* (pp. 181-193). Washington, DC: NASW Press.

Horncastle, J. (1994). Training for international social work: Initial experiences. *International social work*, *37*, 309-320.

Ife, J. (2007). *The new international agenda: What role for social work?* Inaugural Hokenstad international social work lecture. Retrieved from http://ifsw.org/statements/the-new-international-agendas-what-role-for-social-work

Ife, J. (2001). Local and global practice: Relocating social work as a human rights profession in the new global order. *European Journal of Social Work*, 4(1), 5-15.

Ife, J., & L. Morley. (2001). Integrating local and global practice using a human rights framework. Communication presentée lors de la Conférence de l'Association Internationale des Ecoles de Travail Social - Montpellier - France juillet.

Ife, J., & Fiske, L. (2006). Human rights and community work. Complementary theories and practices. *International Social Work*, 49(3), 297-308.

Johannesen, T. (1997). Social work as an international profession. Opportunities and challenges. In M.C.

Hokenstad & J. Midgley (Eds.), *Issues in international social work. Global challenges for a new century* (pp. 146-158). Washington, DC: NASW Press.

Johnson, A.K. (2004). Increasing internationalization in social work programs. *International Social Work, 47*(1), 7-23.

Kealey, D.J. (1990). Cross-cultural effectiveness: A study of Canadian technical advisors overseas. Hull, Canada: CIDA.

Kealey, D.J. (2001). *Cross-cultural effectiveness: A study of Canadian technical advisors overseas.* Ottawa: Canadian Foreign Service Institute.

Klassen, M., Lichtmannegger, S., Barlow, C.A., Schwartz, K., Kreitzer, L., Lacroix, M., Macdonald, L., Klassen, M., & Orjasniemi, T. (2009). Das EU-Kanada Austausch-projekt in der Sozialen Arbeit: Entwicklung, Durchführung und Perspektiven für internationale Praktika. *Sozialarbeit in Österreich (Social Work in Austria), 4*, 29-32.

Kornbeck, J. (2004). Linguistic affinity and achieved geographic mobility: Evidence from the recognition of non-national social work qualifications in Ireland and the UK. *European Journal of Social Work, 7*(2), 143-165.

Kornbeck, J. (2001). Language training for prospective and practising social workers: A neglected topic in social work literature. *British Journal of Social Work, 31*, 307-316.

Kreitzer, L. (2002). MSW international concentration student handbook. Calgary, AB: Faculty of Social Work, University of Calgary. Retrieved from http://www.ucalgary.ca/uofc/faculties/SW/docs/international/isw/MSW

Kreitzer, L. (2006). Social work values and ethics issues of universality. *Currents: New Scholarship in the Human Services, 5*(1). Retrieved from http://fsw.ucalgary.ca/currents/articles/kreitzer_v5_n1.htm

Kreitzer, L., & Wilson, M. (2009). Shifting perspective on international alliances in social work: Lessons from

Ghana and Nicaragua. *International Social Work, 53*(5), 701-19.

Kreitzer, L., Barlow, C.A., Schwartz, K., Lacroix, M., & Macdonald, L. (2012) Canadian and European social work students in a cross-cultural program: What they learned from the experience. *International Social Work, 55*(2), 245-267.

La Brack, B. (2012). Theory connections, reflections and applications for international educators. Notes from the paper *Cultural Adaptation, culture shock and the 'Curves of Adjustment'* given at the NAFSA: Association of International Educators, 63rd Annual conference. Houston, TX.

La détention des mineurs. (2008). Retrieved from http://www.cire.irisnet.be/ouvrons/fr/analyse.html #mineur

Lager, P.Y., & Mathiesen, S. (2012). Bridging social work theory and practice in international field education. In L. Healy & R. Link (Eds.), *Handbook of international social work*. New York, NY: Oxford.

Lager, P., Mathiesen, S., Rogers, M., & Cox, S. (2012) *Guidebook for international field placements and student exchanges: Planning, implementation, and sustainability*. Alexandria, VA: Council on Social Work Education.

Laird, S. (2008). *Anti-oppressive social work: A guide for developing cultural competence*. London: Sage Publications.

Larson, G., & Allen, H. (2006). Conscientization – The experience of Canadian social work students in Mexico. *International Social Work, 49*(4), 507-518.

Levy, D. (2000). Shock of the strange, the shock of the familiar: Learning from study abroad. *Journal of the National Collegiate Honors Council, Spring,* 75-83. Retrieved from http://digitalcommons.unl.edu/nchc journal

Link, R.J., & Vogrincic, G.C. (2012). Models of international exchange. In L.M. Healy & R.J. Link (Eds.), *Handbook of International Social Work* (pp. 343-348). New York, NY: Oxford University Press.

Louie, K. (2005). *Gathering cultural knowledge. Useful or use with care?* In J. Carroll & J. Ryan (Eds.), *Teaching International Students: Improving Learning for All* (pp. 17-25). New York, NY: Routledge.

Lyons, K. (2006). Globalization and social work: International and local implications. *British Journal of social work, 36,* 365-380.

Lyons, K. (2002). Globalisation and education for international social work.   Communication présentée lors de la Conférence de l'Association Internationale des Écoles de Travail Social - Montpellier, France.

Lyons, K.H. (1999). *International Social Work: Themes and Perspectives.* Aldershot, Angleterre: Ashgate.

Lysgaard, S. (1955). Adjustment in a foreign society: Norwegian Fulbright grantees visiting the United States. *International Social Science Bulletin, 7,* 45-51.

Martin, J.N., & Harrell, T. (2004). Intercultural re-entry of student and professionals: Theory and practice. In D. Landis, J.M. Bennett, & M.J. Bennett (Eds.), *Handbook of intercultural training* (pp. 309-336). Thousand Oaks, CA: Sage publications.

McIntosh, P. (1989). White privilege: Unpacking the invisible backpack. *Peace & Freedom.* Retrieved from http://www.library.wisc.edu/edvrc/docs/public/pdfs/LIReadings/InvisibleKnapsack.pdf

Michigan State University. (2012). *Study abroad for gay, lesbian, bisexual, and transgendered (GLBT) students.* Retrieved from http://studyabroad.isp.msu.edu/forms/glbt.html

Midgley, J. (1992). The challenge of international social work. In M.C. Hokenstad, S.K. Khinduka & J. Midgley (Eds.), *Profiles in international social work* (pp. 13-28). Washington, DC: NASW Press.

Midgley, J. (1997). Social work and international social development. Promoting a developemental perspective in the profession". In M.C. Hokenstad & J. Midgley (Eds.), *Issues in international social work. Global challenges for a new century* (pp.11-26). Washington, DC: NASW Press.

Midgley, J. (2001). Issues in international social work: Resolving critical debates in the profession. *Journal of social work, 1*(1), 21-35.

Midgley, J. (2002). Mondialisation, capitalisme et aide sociale: une perspective de développement social, *Travail social canadien. Le travail social et la mondialisation, 2*(1), 13-31.

Nafsa (2011). *Rainbow special interest group (SIG).* Bloomington, IN: Indiana University Office of Overseas Study.

Nagy, G., & Falk, D. (2000). Dilemmas in international and cross-cultural social work education. *International Social Work, 43*(1), 49-60.

Newcomer's guide. (n.d.). *Culture shock and reverse culture shock.* Boston, MA: Massachusetts Institute of Technology. Retrieved from http://newcomers-guide.mit.edu/ng/culture-shock

Oberg, K. (1960). Culture shock: Adjustment to new cultural environment. *Practical Anthropologist, 7,* 177-182.

Payne, M., & Askeland, G. (2008). *Globalization and international social work: Postmodern change and challenge.* Aldershot: Ashgate Publishing Company.

Plateforme Mineurs en exile: La tutelle des mineurs étrangers non accompagnés. (2008). (ou « loi Tabita »). Retrieved from http://www.mena.be/mineurs_en_exil_06.php

Pugh, R. (2003). Understanding language practice, policy and provision in social work. In J. Kornbeck (Ed.), *Language Teaching in Social Work* (pp. 16-38). Mainz: Logophon.

Razack, N. (2000). North/south collaborations: affecting transnational perspectives for social work. *Journal of Progressive Human Services, 11*(1), 71-91.

Razack, N. (2002a). A critical examination of international student exchanges. *International social work, 45*(2), 251-265.

Razack, N. (2002b). *Transforming the field: Critical antiracist and anti-oppressive perspectives for the human services practicum.* Halifax, NS: Fernwood Publishers.

Reichert, E. (2003). *Social and human rights. A foundation for policy and practice.* New York, NY: Columbia University Press.

Rohrlich, B.F., & Martin, J.N. (1991). Host country and re-entry adjustment of student sojourners. *International Journal of Intercultural Relations, 15,* 163-182.

Rowe, W., Hanley, J., Repetur Moreno, E., & Mould J. (2002). Voix de la pratique du travail Social. *Travail social canadien, Le travail social et la mondialisation, 2*(1), 72-97.

Russell-Chapin, L.A. & Ivey, A.E. (2004). *Your supervised practicum and internship: Field resources for turning theory into action.* Belmont CA: Brooks/Cole.

Schon, D.A. (1983). *Reflective practice: How professionals think in action.* New York, NY: Basic Books.

Schwartz, K., & van de Sande A. (2003). Development of an orientation to field practicum for international social work students. *Canadian Association of Schools of Social Work at the Congress of the Social Sciences and Humanities,* Halifax, Nova Scotia.

Schwartz, K., Kreitzer, L., Lacroix, M., Barlow, C.A, Macdonald, L., Lichtmannegger, S., Klassen, M., Orjasniemi, T., & Meunier, D. (2011). Preparing students for international exchanges: Canada/ European Union experiences. *European Journal of Social Work, 14*(3) 421-435.

Sewpaul, V. (2001). Models of intervention for children in difficult circumstances in South Africa. *Child Welfare, 80*(5), 571-586.

Storti, C. (1997). *The art of coming home.* Yarmouth, NS: Intercultural Press.

Stroh, L.K., Gregersen, H.B. & Black, J.S. (1998). Closing the gap: Expectations versus reality among repatriates. *Journal of world business, 33*(2), 111-124.

Sur les méthodes de détermination de l'âge à des fins juridiques. Comité Consultatif National d'Ethique pour les Sciences de la Vie et de la Santé. (2005). Avis n° 88. Deschamps, C., Mandelbaum, J., Ameisen, J.C., Grimfeld, A., Korsia, H., de Rouffignac, C., & Roux, M. Retrieved from http://www.sdj.be/

admin/docmena/MENA_determination_age_CCNEa
vis1.pdf

Sussman, N.M. (1986). Re-entry research and training: Methods and implications. *International Journal of Intercultural Relations, 10,* 235-254.

Szkudlarek, B. (2010). Reentry – A review of literature. *International Journal of intercultural relations, 34,* 1-21.

Tange, H. (2005). In a cultural no man's land or, how long does culture shock last? *Journal of Intercultural Communication, 10.*

Tanner, J.M. & Whitehouse, R.H. (1959). *Standard for skeletal maturity, Part 1.* Paris: International Children's Centre.

Tanner, J.M. & Whitehouse, R.H. (1962). *A new system for estimating skeletal maturity from the hand and wrist, with standards from a study of 2,600 health British children, Part II.* Paris: International Children's Centre.

Thompson, N. (2006). *Anti-discriminatory practice.* Basingstoke: Macmillan.

Three Rivers, A. (1990). *Cultural etiquette: A guide for the well-intentioned.* Cranston, RI: Marketwimmin. Retrieved from http://www.welearnwomen.org

Tourism ethics. (n.d.). *Tourism ethics.* Retrieved from http://resourcepage.gambia.dk/tour_ethics.htm

UNICEF: Nutrition. (2008). Retrieved from http://www.unicef.org/french/nutrition/index.html

van de Sande, A. & Schwartz, K. (2011). *Research for social justice: A community based approach.* Halifax: Fernwood Publishing.

Watt, L. (2005). Critical self-gazing: Education for anti-oppressive practice. *Open Access Dissertations and Theses.* Paper 6369. Retrieved from http://digital-commons.mcmaster.ca/opendissertations/6369

Weaver, G. (1987). The process of re-entry. *Advising Quarterly, 2*(Fall), 1-9.

Westfall de Gurrola, N. (n.d.). Culture shock. Retrieved from http://ww2.odu.edu/ao/oip/studyabroad/resources/culturaladjustment.pdf

Westwood, M.J., Lawrence, W.S. & Paul, D. (1986). Preparing for re-entry: A program for the sojourning student. *International Journal for the Advancement of Counselling, 9,* 221-230.

Wehbi, S. (2009). Deconstructing motivations: Challenging international social work placements. *International Social Work*, *52*(1), 48-59.

Wilfing, H., (2003). Teaching Turkish language and cultural background at the Fachhochshule Campus Wein, Department of Social Work. In J. Kornbeck (Ed.), *Language teaching in social work* (pp. 135-151). Mainz: Logophon.

Wilson, M.G., & Whitmore, E. (2000). *Seeds of fire*. Halifax, NS: Fernwood Publishing.

Yale University (2012). *Re-entry shock*. New Haven, CT: Yale University. Retrieved from http://www.yale.edu/oiss/life/leaving/reentry.html

# Index

CPSIA information can be obtained at www.ICGtesting.com
Printed in the USA
LVOW07s2308031114

411894LV00001B/13/P